Responding to and assessing writing

The NATIONAL *Writing* PROJECT

Nelson

Thomas Nelson and Sons Ltd
Nelson House   Mayfield Road
Walton-on-Thames   Surrey
KT12 5PL   UK

51 York Place
Edinburgh
EH1 3JD   UK

Thomas Nelson (Hong Kong) Ltd
Toppan Building 10/F
22A Westlands Road
Quarry Bay   Hong Kong

Distributed in Australia by

Thomas Nelson Australia
480 La Trobe Street
Melbourne   Victoria 3000
and in Sydney, Brisbane, Adelaide and Perth

© SCDC Publications 1989
First published by Thomas Nelson and Sons Ltd 1989

Photographs: Keith Hawkins, Mike Levers, Alistair MacGregor

ISBN 0-17-424114-3
NPN 98765432
Printed in Great Britain by Bell & Bain Ltd, Glasgow

Acknowledgements

Hundreds of teachers and thousands of children have participated in the National Writing Project. They have been supported by many local advisers, members of higher education colleges, parents and others in the community. We cannot name them all, but we would like to acknowledge the commitment of those participants, and trust that these publications represent at least some of their views about classroom practice.

The National Writing Project was set up by the School Curriculum Development Committee. Its three-year Development Phase (1985-1988) directly involved twenty-four local authorities and it was funded jointly by the School Curriculum Development Committee and the LEAs. In 1988, the National Curriculum Council took responsibility for the Project's final implementation year.

Central Project Team (Development Phase 1985-1988)

Pam Czerniewska: Director

Eve Bearne
Barbara Grayson   } Project Officers
John Richmond
Jeremy Tafler

Naomi Baker
Anne Hogan   } Administrators
Judy Phillips

Central Project Team (Implementation Phase 1988-1989)

Jeremy Tafler: Director

Georgina Herring   } Project Officers
Marie Stacey

Rosemary Robertson: Administrator

Steering Committee

Andrew Wilkinson: Chair

Dennis Allen
Peter Andrews
Iain Ball
Douglas Barnes
Eunice Beaumont
Harold Gardiner
Alan Hall
David Halligan
John Johnson
Gulzar Kanji
Keith Kirby
Maggie Maclure
June Thexton
Jenny Taylor
Mike Torbe
Janet White

Local Project Co-ordinators

Avon	Richard Bates
Bedfordshire	Mary Heath
Berkshire	Audrey Gregory
	Barry Pope
Birmingham	Ann Davis
	Sylvia Winchester
Cheshire	Gill Fox
	John Huddart
Cleveland	Margaret Meek
	Joan Sedgewicke
Croydon	Sheila Freeman
	Iain Weir
Dorset	Barbara Tilbrook
	Margaret Wallen
Dudley	Chris Morris
Durham	Dot Yoxall
Gwynedd	Len Jones
	Esyllt Maelor
	Nia Pierce Jones
Hampshire	Robin Culver
	Cath Farrow
	Ann Heslop
	Roger Mulley
Humberside	Sylvia Emerson
ILEA	Helen Savva
Manchester	Helen Henn
	Georgina Herring
Mid Glamorgan	Richard Landy
Newcastle	Jay Mawdsley
Rochdale	Frances Clarke
	Peter Phethean
	Vivienne Rowcroft
SCEA	Stuart Dyke
Sheffield	Sue Horner
Shropshire	Ned Ratcliffe
Somerset	Vernon Casey
	Maisie Foster
	Carole Mason
Staffordshire	Sallyanne Greenwood
Wiltshire	Gill Clarkson
	Sue Dean
	Jo Stone

Contents

Ways of looking at children's writing: The National Writing Project
response to the Task Group on Assessment and Testing (TGAT)

Introduction

This collection of articles is about responses to writing — each response being a vehicle for feedback about how effective a piece of writing has been. In the accounts, teachers relate some ideas, strategies and changes of perception that they have experienced, working across the age range and throughout the curriculum. We hope that these may encourage readers to question aspects of their own practice in order to facilitate the development of their pupils' confidence and competence in writing.

Many hundreds of teachers involved in the National Writing Project have been considering responses to writing. While there are some differences in their conclusions, a broad consensus has emerged. Aspects of this are as follows:

Response should encourage

Everyday writing tasks generally receive a response by which we gauge their success. The shopping list does or does not do its job; the lesson plan precedes good or bad pupil reaction; the letter to the newspaper does or does not get published. In the classroom, many writing tasks do not have this immediate relevance to the world of the writer. The main audience is often perceived to be the teacher, and the response a correction or comment written at the end of a piece of work, perhaps with a red pen, perhaps executed in the absence of the child and perhaps nothing more than a tick, grade or mark.

Children are resilient. Most are anxious to please. But what they (and we) require is a supportive, interested and relevant reaction if they are to continue to see writing as something useful and worthwhile.

Response can come from a variety of sources

There is a wealth of opportunity for others to respond to our pupils' writing. Many examples are given in the case studies — classmates, older and younger children, family, friends, local media, the local community. If the writing task has real purpose, the success of a piece of writing should be apparent by the effect that it has on its audience. Did anyone buy the magazine? Did the Infants like the story? Could they make the cakes from the recipe? Did the rest of the class understand the experiment? Did they find the literature notes useful?

Serious writing deserves a serious response which engages with what the writer is trying to say and how the writer is saying it, as well as how well it conforms to writing conventions.

An audience cannot respond without thinking about the purpose of the piece. If the purpose were merely to satisfy the demands of the teacher, we must expect a level of engagement in and commitment to the task commensurate with that. Thinking about the nature of response necessarily involves asking questions about the nature of the task.

It is helpful if writers have thought through the nature of the response that they require. Do I want suggestions? Am I asking whether the writing is developing along the right lines? Is the 'voice' right? Is the spelling correct? Am I fulfilling the needs of the reader? Am I including too little/too much information to make my meaning clear?

Response may suggest how the writing may be improved by the writer

Mere correction is seldom as effective.

We cannot learn *for* our pupils. They must reflect on their activities and react if they are to build on their experiences. Even in the area of spelling, it is rare for young writers to be unable to identify the words about which they are unsure. All response implies some sort of assessment. If that assessment is available during the writing as well as at the end, new perceptions can be incorporated into the developing piece. When we are allowed freedom to experiment, we realise that mistakes are useful in that they can be learned from, and we do not need to fear them.

Response and assessment

This pack does not provide yardsticks which can be applied to pieces of work to measure their quality, nor does it map developmental routes taken by developing writers on their way to some defined goal.

This is not to say that the Project Team underestimates the importance of being able to assess a piece of writing and to justify that assessment. There are times when it is appropriate to make judgements, and it is necessary that the criteria for these judgements are known to both teacher and pupil. The National Writing Project submission to the Task Group on Assessment and Testing is appended; it makes points which we believe should be borne in mind in the formulation of national assessment strategies. The Project's argument is that criteria for assessment should be reconstructed by each teacher and group of pupils. The proof of good criteria is that using them will tend to reinforce the best classroom practice.

The case studies and activities that follow are divided into five sections. Section One offers some teachers' and pupils' perceptions of the nature of response and some ideas about how the teacher might intervene.

Section Two deals with the opportunities for writers within a class to work together in order to receive immediate feedback from each other.

Section Three indicates some audiences outside the classroom.

Section Four looks at how young writers become self-critical, evaluating their own learning and writing by absorbing their readers' comments.

Section Five looks at ways of encouraging teachers, parents and other interested parties to reflect on current approaches.

Teachers' comments

'Some of the material I used as it stands, taking ideas and trying them as they were suggested, the log books for example. Other ideas, such as the questionnaires, I adapted to suit the age and abilities of my own children.'

The case studies represent snapshots in teachers' development; many of the authors have moved on in their thinking since the time of writing. Readers, too, may look at the work and find new questions arising. One significant area may be the sensitive intervention required in probing assumptions about gender and racial stereotypes while maintaining children's sense of authorship.

Response is a complex area and cannot be looked at without considering the whole writing environment. This chart is offered as a basis for thought.

Responding to children's writing

Why is it that after we have organised our classroom into a community of readers and writers, engrossed in real tasks, genuinely communicating with people, that when the writing is done we still find ourselves reaching for the red pen? What range of responses is the young writer entitled to? Where does assessment fit into this?

Are we exploiting all the possibilities for helpful responses to writing?

BACKGROUND CONSIDERATIONS

What are we responding to?
how was the writing initiated?
what is the intention of the piece?
what stage is the piece at?
who is the intended audience?
what is the intended *form* of the writing (letter, report, argument)?
what is the intended *function* (to amuse, to inform, to persuade)?

What are the writer's needs?
what sort of response does the writer want?
what experience does the writer have of different responses?
what's important – ideas? appropriateness for audience? surface features? overall structure . . . ?
. . . and what aspects of the work can be left? will intervention at this point do any good?

What general constraints are there?
what were the constraints on writing (time, resources)?
what are the constraints on responding (school policy, parents'/society's demands)?
are these constraints fixed or mutable? Are pupils aware of them?

WHY?

Is the response intended
to motivate?
to provide a sounding board for ideas?
to share a task?
to point out problems that stand in the way of ultimate success?
to suggest an external measure of success or failure?
to provide feedback?

WHEN?

Is the response
at the beginning? to get the ideas sorted out?
in the middle? how is it progressing? Is it suited to its audience? Is it doing what the writer hopes? Is it worth doing? Is it worth continuing?
at the end? Is it interesting? Has it achieved its desired effect? What can be learned for next time?

HOW?

Is the response
spoken?
written? in ink? pencil? on the child's work? on a separate sheet?
some other action?

Consider whether the message changes with the medium of the response. Are you more sympathetic, for example, when you respond orally? How do you decide which is the most useful type of response?

WHO IS RESPONDING?

the writer?
if we want our pupils to be able to evaluate their own work, they can only learn to do it through practice. What strategies give more responsibility to the writer?

their peers?
how can we help young writers to make helpful responses to each others' work? Can we use worklogs? journals? a vocabulary with which to talk about writing? modelling by teacher?

older/younger children?
easily accessible audience with differing demands

a wider audience?
the community, parents, the media, examination boards . . .

the teacher?
as sympathetic reader?
as critic?
as assessor?

Does the pupil recognise your changing role?

WHO IS THE RESPONSE FOR?

the pupil?
who may discover how her writing can improve.

the teacher?
who may learn the success/failure of previous strategies and point the way to new ones.

outside agencies?
including parents, other teachers, new schools, employers, who may need a different sort of information.

HOW WAS IT EXPLAINED?

to pupils?
to parents?
to other teachers?

WHAT NEXT?

develop?
polish?
put away?
publish?
display?
throw away?

Look back over your comments on children's work – what impression would they have of what is important to you? If you ask them what is important in writing, what do they say? – is it what you hoped? Where did they get the ideas from? How would you change them?

'To get it marked' is not much of a reason for writing. Teachers deserve a better fate than to be seen as simply assessors of their pupils' writing.

Are we, as teachers, spending time on tasks that either the children or someone else should be doing?

Consultative Group

Richard Bates
Frances Clarke
Maisie Foster
Sheila Freeman
Ned Ratcliffe
Lucy Scott-Ashe
Jeremy Tafler

With thanks to all the teachers, children and parents whose work is represented here.

Special acknowledgement needs to be given to those teachers who responded to the early drafts, in particular the trialling groups in the Isle of Man, the Isle of Wight, Lancashire, North Yorkshire and West Sussex.

1 Perceptions of response

> The marking at my primary school was not very helpful. The teachers wrote coments at the end like good or see me or something like that. I used to get really annoyed when they wrote something like good and left you wondering what good really meant.
>
> Catherine Green
> 2k

What do we think about response?

Children do have perceptions about the role of writing, and they do not always match the ideas which teachers expect or wish them to have. They tend to give priority to surface features — spelling, grammar and neatness. Proficiency in these conventions is, of course, important; the need for competence in the technical aspects of writing is not questioned. However, if the surface features are all that the children perceive as important, teachers cannot be surprised if their children's work lacks the other qualities that they seek. Teachers often feel uneasy about the responses they make but are not sure what to put in their place.

A boy wrote a poem

NICHOLAS CHAPMAN

A boy wrote a poem,
It was from homework from class,
He wrote about cliff-tops,
And how the winds pass.
He just let it flow
from his head to his pen,
But his spelling was bad,
"C, do this again!"

A boy wrote a poem,
And thought of his mark.
And this time he checked it
And wrote of the dark.
He changed and corrected,
Gave it in the next day,
He got "B+ Good effort"
and threw it away.

When he wrote of the oceans,
They gave him an "E".
They gave him an "E"
for the tides of the sea,
"What does it mean?"
Said the boy to his work,
"Does it mean I'm just lazy,
Does it mean I'm a berk?"

When he wrote about sunrise,
They gave him an "A".
They gave him an "A"
for the dawn of the day,
"What does this mean?"
Said the boy to his paper,
"Am I meant to be happy,
To leap up, cut a caper?"

"What is this letter?
It is nothing to me!
It doesn't mention the good bit
At the end of verse three"
And so thought the boy,
But he couldn't be sure,
So he looked at his shoes
And the tiles on the floor.

Then, before long,
At a certain time,
They asked for the marks
of the efforts in rhyme.
To be written down
In a large orange book,
In symmetrical lines,
To be read at one look.

And he sat at the back,
At the back of the room,
Among the new novels,
The display work, the gloom.
And they asked him his marks,
And he read them ashamed,
When he got to his worst
"Tut,tut," they exclaimed.

Oh, he thought.
But I don't see what those marks have
got to do with my work.

He still doesn't understand.

The Cheshire Writing Project has concentrated on children's perceptions of response. Gill Fox used this short questionnaire.

'What do you like (dislike) to happen to your writing:

- to be displayed?
- to be read out?
- to be kept in a folder?
- something else?

Why?

What do you feel about reading or listening to other people's writing?
Why?

How do you like the teacher to mark your work?

What sort of comments are helpful/unhelpful?

Pleasant/unpleasant?

What do you not like?'

Teachers' comments

'Year One [Secondary] pupils enjoyed the opportunity to voice their opinions. At first they worried about the confidentiality of their comments — but then became brutally honest! My response was one of surprise at how private they wished their work to be and how much control they wanted over who saw their work and to what use it was put. I felt almost privileged to read it.'

'The majority wanted their work:

- *to be given a mark*
- *to be marked in red pen so that mistakes would stand out*
- *to have every mistake corrected*
- *to be given a helpful comment*

Most pupils did not wish to have work displayed or published; embarrassment was given as the main reason. It was obvious, however, from the replies that an unjustified lack of confidence in their writing ability prevailed.'

Talking about assessment

I acquired my formal marking style along with my PGCE . . . I became an expert in the field of red pens. No medieval monk lavished more care on his marginalia than I did during my first months . . .

Eight months in . . .

Eight months into the Writing Project, what is the difference in my writing style? Whereas formerly I scored in symbols indicating errors in convention with a firm, bold red pen, now I trace them with the most delicate, hesitant of touches. This may not look like a major step, but it represents more than a change of pressure when applying pen to paper. Before, I did not question; now, I do, but not having any alternative marking strategies, I ease off — and mark time. Another system has to evolve.

I used to have enormous doubts about whether I was improving the quality of the pupils' grasp of writing conventions by marking formally, but it was expected of me, so I did it. The really important work was about building on and delighting in the felicitous phrase, the appropriate tone, the pleasing rhythms which the children captured. This was done by 'talk and write'.

Nearly all the preparatory work was done on scrap paper, with final copies made for display from the fair copy in the child's exercise book. In the course of this we would talk and talk. Then the scrap paper was relegated to the bin. The children

Two teachers — a Secondary English teacher and a Primary teacher — talk about the ways in which their views of response have developed.

had no record of the writing process and little awareness of the nature of their participation in it. The neat exercise book, with its red ink correction, was a totally misleading document. It did not record one half of what the child had put into the production of any particular piece of writing. The more successful children produced material which pleased and surprised us both. If you ask me how, I would say it was because the source material was good, and we were enjoying ourselves. But I found it much more difficult to inspire the less successful children to improve upon their performance. The marking system I employed could take no credit for the brighter children's pieces, and must take some of the blame for the failures.

So after eight months some children are using the magic line (where a child puts a dash instead of a word if uncertain about its spelling). This is proving to be a liberating device, increasing the chances a child will take when striving for expression. The children are involved in spotting mistakes and assessing the effect of the writing. The concept of 'rough' is banned from my own and my pupils' minds and vocabularies. The 'best' book is a thing of the past. The exercise book is the working record.

I used to think (if I thought at all, which I doubt) of the individual child learning what I had to offer. Now I see the children and myself engaged much more in a joint enterprise. I know I used to talk too much: be too informative. I am now much more likely to be found pondering in public or with individuals, or asking questions, or, of course, writing alongside children.

Eighteen months in . . .

I clung to the old crutches until the following autumn. With the falling of the red leaves, so fell the red pen. There followed a period of invention and discovery, negotiating and sharing. All classes were involved in thinking, talking, listening and writing lessons which had the potential for publication or performance, and new methods of assessment and classroom management had to follow.

With the second year children, we pushed out the Ark and floated into uncharted waters on three chapters of Genesis. We gathered extracts from 'Mrs. Noah's Diary', 'recovered' Mr. Noah's notebook about the structure of the Ark (complete with simple working drawings) and created personal poems, hymns of thanksgiving for deliverance, and anecdotes real or imagined. The Art and Music departments joined in too, but that's another story. We crowned our term's work with a huge display, and a seven-scene, half-hour performance of the Flood drama.

Meanwhile, the first year children were being investigative journalists on Flannan Isle, and the third year children were constructing records of villages (which they had invented) with all the zest of latter-day Plantagenet monarchs. The GCSE classes still attended closely to texts, from which they made their meanings with little help from me. They wrote as widely and as deeply as they were able, and were given plenty of time to concentrate on their source material and on the writing process. All began to think of themselves and to refer to themselves as writers.

What was going on in my classroom was being repeated throughout the whole department, and thanks to the positive attitude of the heads of Science and Humanities, creative writing was creeping across the curriculum.

We decided that it was essential to involve the parents, and in the summer of 1987 we held a special evening (under the auspices of the PTFA) to explain why children would no longer be coming home with neat books full of individual exercises nicely ticked and marked out of ten.

Parents listened attentively, seemed impressed by the displays, and were reassured that the surface features had been attended to. The most frequently voiced comment was, '*I wish it had been like this when I was at school.*'

Errors in the mechanics of writing are now treated as evidence of learning, of attempts at using conventions, rather than as something which requires surgical treatment. Written work which falls below an acceptable standard is returned as 'unread' and the child is invited to say why the piece is as it is. The tone of the response here should be 'more in sorrow than in anger'!

No child now has a mark at the end of a piece of written work; but there is always a comment. At the end of each half term we ask the pupils to write us a brief report about how they see their own progress, or what difficulties or pleasures have been encountered. We then give each child a brief written assessment. In addition, the Lower School classes receive silver stars for work which is particularly pleasing or promising. Teachers may decide how to keep their own mark book, as long as it provides a sound record of progress.

I used to feel overwhelmed by the sheer number of 'them' in relation to me. Since adopting many of the ideas developed by the National Writing Project I have felt far less overwhelmed. I do less formal marking than previously. The children hand in their books less frequently because they spend more time over fewer pieces of writing. This does not mean that I work less hard, but it certainly is the case that I have never enjoyed teaching more than I do now. I hope that I'm getting it right.

Jane Doonan, Avon Writing Project Support Group

Have a go!

Since the beginning of the Writing Project I think the biggest change in my attitude to the children's writing has been in the approach I take to marking. I now try to approach the work in a far more positive way, looking for good points to praise rather than faults. The thing I have found especially interesting has been the children's unexpected ability to spell for themselves.

During 'free writing' sessions I used to make the children put up their hands for spellings and I then went to each of them in turn to put the words in their word books. This put a great deal of pressure on me to get round as fast as I could, and I also feel that this method slowed down and even broke a child's train of thought.

Recently I have tried a different approach. I told the children that during the session I would not give them any words. They must concentrate on what they wanted to write and make their own attempts at spelling. This idea was received with horror and groans. Several children tried to persuade me at various times during the session to give them spellings but I refused. During the second session I again said that no spellings would be given. There were fewer groans and no attempt to persuade me to spell words, and the children seemed to be more involved in what they were writing. Since the second session the children have not been asking about spellings. They have accepted the approach much more readily than I would have expected.

What has surprised me most is that this approach has actually led to a marked improvement in the children's spelling. I did not realise just how well they could spell without my aid. I now feel I was holding them back and not giving them the confidence needed to attempt their own spellings. They had more experience and knowledge than they or I had realised. It is especially significant that this improvement was seen in the majority of the children, representing a wide range of abilities.

Sue Allen, St. James C. of E. School, Handsworth, Birmingham

Teachers' comments

'I tried this refusal to give spellings during free writing and was surprised at the number of children who could spell quite well without my help. Some of them had been far too dependent upon me and lacked confidence, but when they realised there was no terrible punishment for wrong spellings, they were happy to "have a go".'

For discussion

When we respond to a child's writing, whether orally or on paper, we are probably addressing several different aspects of the writing at once. What are they? Here are some examples of responses to different aspects:

- surface features

  'sp'; 'I can't really read this, could you read it for me?' — proof reading, adjusting punctuation and generally editing the writing so it conforms to the conventions of adult writing

- style and structure

  'I liked this word'; 'Good use of vocabulary'; 'Check the verb agreement here'; 'You need an introduction to help the reader'; 'This bit is particularly clear'; 'This is lucid but you didn't really keep the very young audience in mind despite the fact that you were alerted to it at the revising stage.'

- ideas and content

  'What happened next?'; 'Abbott is interesting on this'; 'What about Robespierre?'; 'What is your evidence for this?'

- the writer as a writer

  'I thought your brainstorm was full of interesting ideas but you didn't really develop these despite good advice from your writing group.'

- the writer as a person

  'Well done, Jane'; 'What a shame about your dog'; 'I really enjoyed reading this'; 'It's clear that you understand acid rain — if you could ask the Prime Minister one question relating to the political aspects of pollution, what would it be?'; 'Your account of working in a cinema was hilarious and you seem to have the gift of making people laugh — can you tell jokes too?'

Which aspects do we address most often? Which do we neglect? Check through some of your children's exercise books to see which may appear to concern you most.

How and when should the teacher intervene?

Teachers can build potential response into writing tasks by the way in which the tasks are set up and the context in which they are set. If the children have had some control over the tasks, their feedback can come from sources other than the teacher. In many Primary school classrooms there is a writing corner, supplied with a variety of paper, writing instruments and other stationery, where the children can go by choice to do their own writing. Consider this piece, found in such a corner in an Infant classroom.

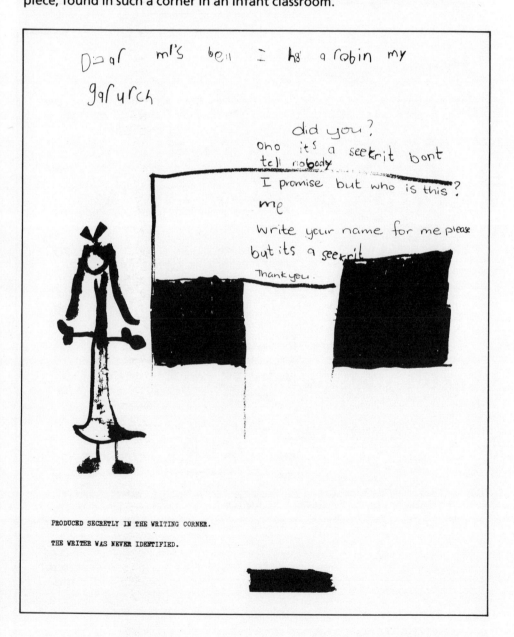

Dear mrs ben I has a robin my garurch

did you?
oho its a seekrit bont tell nobody
I promise but who is this?
me
write your name for me please
but its a seekrit
Thankyou.

PRODUCED SECRETLY IN THE WRITING CORNER.

THE WRITER WAS NEVER IDENTIFIED.

Compare this with these sentences produced by a seven-year-old to satisfy a nightly homework demand for seven sentences.

My ~~grampa~~ Grandfather has ~~got~~ bees in his garden

I ~~have~~ *had* some jelly ~~for~~ *at* a party

I eat my tea ~~up~~

My mum teaches me Chess.

Some people cannot ~~not~~ smell gas

My cousin (fails) *failed his/her* driving test ~~s~~

There are *twenty four* 24 hours in a day

When ~~it~~ *it* snows the windows are frosty. *it* ... *n do* ... *fr*

is this or? of? →
A packet of crisps some *I cannot read this* M=ms, fruit pastiles and chewing gum costs 40p all together

Teachers have frequently asked, *'When can I be sure that intervention is necessary?'* and *'In what ways can I most effectively intervene?'*

When teachers respond to a piece of writing, it is helpful if they make their implicit criteria explicit, so that children can more fully understand what they are being asked to do when they are asked to write. If teachers are confident that their instinctive reactions to children's writing are the right ones, they should be able to articulate the reasons. Merely to tick a piece of work and add a comment such as *'Good work'* is not a helpful response unless the writer is told what is good about the writing. Children should not be expected to try and guess what teachers are thinking. If the writing has a purpose, if there is a reason for doing it, it is incumbent upon teachers to make clear comments about its effectiveness.

Most of what children need to know about writing is learned by experience: of talking, listening, reading and writing. This learning is constant, very powerful, and mainly unconscious. No child can learn to write without such experience. It works from the little — where to put commas in sentences — to the large — what are the characteristics of a successful piece of factual explanation, or narrative, or argument? This learning does not happen in a linear, incremental fashion. Writing development seems to follow a learning spiral, with children visiting and revisiting an area and improving their performance each time. The teacher's major job is to provide circumstances in which these rich experiences can happen and to intervene in ways that will help children to build on each literacy event.

When teachers respond to writing they are modelling a range of strategies that writers can use to help each other, and developing with them a vocabulary with which to talk about and understand writing. Through responses to writing, we can show young writers how different readers react to a piece of writing and, over time, develop 'the reader within the writer' — the ability to judge one's own work.

'. . . writers need a genuine response which attends to the whole of what has been written. The response, written or spoken, must be an exchange in long-running conversation between teacher and child. The conversation can be business-like. Genuine response is not the same as scattering praise like confetti.'[1]

[1] John Richmond: 'The class as a community of writers' from *Ways of Looking: Issues from the National Writing Project* (Nelson)

TEACH BY ILLUSTRATION NOT ABSTRACT DEFINITION

TURN IMPLICIT KNOWLEDGE INTO EXPLICIT OPERATIONS

INTERVENTION SHOULD

SEE PATTERN IN ERROR

SIGNIFY A REAL READER

Illustration not definition

Children don't learn how to control an element of writing by being given definitions and rules. Definitions and rules are abstractions, attempts to analyse reality. There is nothing wrong with analysis, but analysis comes *after* competence, not before. Children learn by seeing examples of how other writers have used speech marks or paragraphs, or discussed a controversial issue, or described a scientific process. 'Other writers' should include other children and ourselves, as well as published writers.

Implicit knowledge/explicit operations

Children know more about writing than they know that they know. Their implicit understanding of an element of writing – the understanding they have from all their other experiences of language – is in advance of their ability regularly and reliably to control that element under the pressure of production. The teacher appeals to that implicit understanding in asking the learner to perform a conscious operation on the text; to be a critic or a detective. 'We've got a bit of a problem with the marking of sentences – with full stops and capital letters. There are about six places on this page where you haven't marked the sentences right. Can you find them?' They can find most of them.

Pattern in error

There is no such person as a writer, however unsuccessful, whose writing is just a mass of ignorance and confusion. There are always a few things – maybe no more than two or three – which are causing the major difficulties. The teacher's skill is in looking past the superficial symptoms, seeing the pattern in the error, and attending with the child to the two or three things which matter most now.

Real readers

The key is the context: when children are engaged in writing for a purpose they understand and an audience they care about, they are usually determined to get the conventions right too. The single most important principle of intervention is that teachers must behave as real readers; our first reaction must be to what writing is telling us.

Early writers

> ## For discussion
>
> Here is a piece of work from a five-year-old called Louise. It reads:
>
> *'Monday 14th September. On Saturday I got my dog and she is called Phoebe.'*
>
>
>
> What would be the functions of the following responses?
>
> - *'Good girl, Louise.'*
> - ✓
> - *'Lucky you! My dog is called Sophie.'*
> - writing in *'-aturday', '-he', '-alled', 'Phoebe'*
> - pinning it up on the wall unmarked
> - pinning it up on the wall corrected in some way
> - pinning it up on the wall with a transcription underneath
> - some other response

The Avon Writing Project's Infant manual gives the following advice:

'When talking to children try to:

- *listen to the child*
- *respond to content first*
- *feed back to them what you like about their writing*
- *follow, don't lead*

- *handle one problem at a time*

- *keep the discussion short*

Tell me about your piece of writing.
What part do you like best?
Is there anything you want to add?
Can you tell me more about it?
Are you happy with your beginning and ending?
Is this piece of writing like anything else you've written? Why?
How does this draft sound when you read it aloud?
Is there anything you need help with?
What do you intend to do with this draft?
How did you feel when this happened?
What is the most important thing you are trying to say?'

A positive response will show children that their first attempts at communicating on paper will be taken seriously. They should be asked to share this writing if they want to.

Teacher: *'That looks interesting. Tell me about it.'*
Child: *'It's a comic.'*
Teacher: *'What's happening in your comic?'*

As the writing develops, more extending questions can be used:

wednesday 30th April

my bt- hs pop' and my bt d-m-
and the n- W- s-t

Balloons do make a loud noise

Steven chant

'My balloon has popped and my balloon did move and the noise was so loud.'
'Did it make you jump?'

Nayana

I done handwriing and I am in
Mrs Davies klasand wi þi w-
anþ wi þi mas and to si ve-
h-and my teɔ-is ve nis
I done q qat tɔ go-onthe w-
and wi gog qn It P-

'I done handwriting and I am in Mrs. Davies' class and we do maths and it is very nice. I done a painting to go on the wall and we go out to play.'

'Yes, that was a lovely picture. I like you being in my class. Do you like the Maths being hard?'

The teacher responded first to content and then to surface features:

'What a good try with "class" and "teacher". You've got nearly all the letters and you found the word "handwriting".' (Nayana copied the word 'handwriting' from a drawer.)

Older children

Responding to the surface features — spelling and punctuation — is easy. Any literate adult can do it and indeed many do make that level of response to their own children's writing. A question which teachers must face is, *'How does my own response develop and extend the children's understanding of what they have accomplished in their writing, in a way that the limited and superficial reaction to writing never can?'* It is not a comfortable question to face because it soon becomes clear that the sort of response required by developing writers is one that takes more time and is harder to make. Views on correct sequencing, quality of ideas and suitability of expression become increasingly more subjective than the simple *'You've spelled this wrongly'*. The ground is now less secure.

And yet, if teachers don't know what they are looking for, if they cannot decide, with some degree of consensus, what a 'good' piece of writing is, or rather what are the good aspects of a piece of writing, how are they to claim to be effective guides and facilitators in the classroom?

Teachers can model writing for specific purposes: the report, the argument for and against nuclear power; they can show examples which do their job well, be it to persuade, affect, amuse, attack; they can point out where they think that a piece of writing has lost its way. It is important, though, to go one step further and to make explicit their own criteria for judging pieces of work.

What is involved is a widening of teachers' vocabulary in the classroom, so that they can talk with children about what makes a reader judge a particular piece of writing as fulfilling, or not fulfilling, its function. What makes a piece of writing persuasive? arousing? informative? What could be said to a pupil to demonstrate that one set of notes was more effective than another; or that a piece of writing achieved its purpose of arguing the case for capital punishment? Teachers need frameworks for judging and responding to a piece of writing, frameworks which have developed through discussions with pupils.

In Avon, groups of teachers have been considering how such criteria for responding to texts can be developed by teachers. Low-scoring samples from the Assessment of Performance Unit's survey of eleven-year-olds' writing[2] provoked discussion of what makes an effective piece of persuasive writing. The following activities, using these samples, were presented to Avon teachers. (They are based on INSET materials compiled by Janet White from the National Foundation for Educational Research.)

Activity 1

Think of a subject about which you have a strong opinion. The choice of subject is up to you. Write about it in some detail so as to persuade somebody who does not share your opinion to change their mind, and see things your way.

Spend about twenty minutes on this activity.

Activity 2

Read the following pieces of children's writing (or a selection), jot down your immediate response to them and mark them in your usual way.

1. '*It would be wonderful if the IRA, INLA and the UDA, would stop booming home's and other people's property and tostop killings and kidnapping. Like the two yuear old girl who was kidnapped from her home on friday night she was in her caught sleeping.*

   She was found some miles away from her home dead. and that's why I would like Ireland to be peaceful then more people would come too Ireland than there would be no viliss to fear.'

2. '*The subject that I have a strong opinion is throwing rubbish on the sand at sea-shoars. I have a strong opinion against it because every time I go to the sea I see rubbish on the sand and I see people and children throwing rubbish on the sand like crisps packets and biscit wrappers and orange drink bottels bean thrown on the sand. Sometimes I see children picking up glass botels and smashing them all agains the rocks and stones. If inisant people were walking along happily ready for a swim bear-footed and then suddenly the child or small baby or It could be one of the parents putting their foot on a sharp peace of glass and have a veary bad cut on their foot and prahaps if the baby steped on it the baby might have to go to ahospital because babies skil in much much softer than peoples skin and it could be sirious. If small babies were brought to the beach about a year old and saw a wrapper or something or a piece of glass and picket it up and put it in their mouth without the mother or father watching the baby.*'

---

[2] *Language Performance in Schools: A Review of APU Language Monitoring 1979–1983* (HMSO 1987)

3. '*Fish are very intaining You can have many kinds of fish You can have a flat fish and you can have a peach and a hering and you can have sokedhering wish is a copatp and you can have very many fish they are all dent cant of fish.*'

4. '*I feel verry strong when I argue with my nan or grandad when I want my record player on and they say no. I start to argue and argue untill they say no and when I say no I mean no but I still argue and argue but they take no notice but arfter a while They say no again but I want my own way so I keep on arguing until they say yes so I go to my room and I switch it on and they say I have it on to loud but I do not turn it down because I like music.*'

5. '*I don't like girls play football because there weak and fat and if it was male v female we'll would have to be very gentle.*

   Why do men have more sports than boy an girl.

   I think that boy's should not play with doll's because boy's schold play with A ton man and girl's play with dolls.'

Activity 3

You should respond to the questions in this activity in the order in which they appear.

a What difficulties were there in marking the texts?
What else do you need to know about the writing or writers before you could respond more effectively?

b If you had to rank the texts, in which order would you place them in terms of the writers' ability to construct a persuasive text?

c Drawing on your own piece of persuasive writing and the sample texts, try to make some general statements about what you would expect of writing which is attempting to persuade. What does each writer know about persuasive writing?

Responses to and comments on Activity 3a:

*'It would be easier to respond to the texts . . .
. . . if I knew how old the writers were'*

This reaction is frequently heard, but age is not necessarily a good indicator of a child's writing ability relating to a specific task. Within any age group there will be wide variations in ability, depending on a child's experience and knowledge of the writing demands of a particular task.

'. . . if I knew how this writing compared to other writing produced by these children. If it was the best/worst piece ever produced then clearly this would provoke very different responses from me'

'. . . if I knew more about the children, more about their likely reactions to my response'

Both these typical comments reflect a desire to know more about the history of the writer. Such knowledge is important in helping writers develop their writing skills but not crucial in the objective assessment of a piece of writing.

'. . . if I knew under what conditions the writing had been done — at home, in detention, after a discussion — what sort of stimulus, if any, the children had been given'

'. . . if I knew whether this was a first draft or a revised and edited piece ready for publication'

It is very important that teachers are aware of the stage that a piece of writing has reached, and respond accordingly. A first draft may be little more than a brainstorm of ideas, without the polish of a final draft.

'. . . if I knew what the writing task was. What was the point of the writing? What was it trying to achieve? For whom was it written? What was the teacher's purpose in setting it?'

A teacher can respond much more effectively to writing if both teacher and writer are aware of the purpose of the writing and the audience for which it is intended. (The specific task given to the children in this case was the same one as in Activity 1.)

Responses to and comments on Activity 3c:

'The writing should contain strong feelings which reflect a commitment to the subject. You don't convince someone to change their mind if they sense you don't really believe what you are saying.'

'There has to be a good collection of facts and details so the reader is aware you are someone who knows about the subject, a sort of authority who can be relied on.'

'It should be lively and direct. Boring people doesn't convince them; they switch off.'

'It should take a moral position.'

'It should be logical and well argued with a clear opening . . . development of ideas . . . and concluding remark which also extends the argument.'

'It should appeal to the audience at which it is directed, anticipate responses and answer them.'

'It should show empathy.'

'It should show experience of the subject.'

'There should be a rhetorical use of language (cunning concealment of the truth!)'

'The style and structure should be suited to the purpose.'

'There should be a forceful, punchy argument.'

'It should have visual impact and look good on the page.'

Many of these comments, while easily agreed with, beg further questions. To get the response that your writing should be lively, punchy or empathetic says little about how to make your writing these things. There is a need to extend the vocabulary used in the response so that the writer can see which language structures actually create punch or empathy. For example, we can compare the overall development of the five pieces of writing as persuasive texts:

Text 1 has used an effective structure which begins with a general statement, follows this with a specific example and then sums up the case. There is an overall cohesion to the writing.

Text 2 begins similarly with an opening general statement followed by examples. However, the trail of examples reaches no conclusion, and there is no overall structure.

Text 3, after its opening *'Fish are very entertaining'*, has the structure of a list. All the sentences are similar, beginning *'You can . . .'*

Text 4 has an overall narrative structure with its chronological sequence of events. While narrative forms can be persuasive, the writer's intention here seems to be to relate an event rather than to persuade someone.

Text 5 is particularly interesting as there is no recognisable overall text structure. Rather, there are three separate starting points which are not clearly connected to each other apart from their common theme of 'boys versus girls'.

All these writers seem to be struggling to find a form of writing that will serve to persuade their audience. Is this due to a lack of adequate models — insufficient experience of reading and using persuasive texts?

Observations can also be made about the children's grammatical choices which reveal their knowledge of language devices that persuade. In Text 1 there is some very effective language — structures which produce a punch. For example, in *'she was in her cot sleeping'* and *'she was found some miles away from her home dead'*, the interruption of the main clause with the adverbial phrase increases the impact of each sentence by placing the words *'sleeping'* and *'dead'* at the end. An effective device.

The writer of Text 4 attempts a lively structure in his quotation from his grandparents, *'and when I say no I mean no'*, though his indecision about direct or indirect speech mars the effect.

Text 5 includes a question, which is a useful rhetorical device in an argument.

These few observations about the five texts, looking at the overall text structure and at the grammatical structures employed, illustrate the kinds of thing which teachers might comment on to demonstrate the strengths of particular pieces of writing. Other areas of interest might be vocabulary choice and conventions of spelling and punctuation.

Such responses may help develop in the child a sense of the choices which writers must make each time they write: how shall I try to persuade someone — by an argument, a story, a poem? How will my message have most impact — by asking questions; by changing normal word order? What words should I use?

It is not being recommended here that detailed analyses of texts should take place. However, it may be helpful for teachers to point out and discuss strategies which have been particularly effective, so that a sensitivity to language potential can develop.

2 Response from peers

In this section teachers examine more closely how to involve the whole class in the writing process, as a community of writers, readers and responders.

Children need not be isolated, struggling alone with their thoughts when they are part of a community of writers. Members of this community share a great many experiences and feelings — successes, defeats, humour, anger, pressure and relief.

In an atmosphere of trust and friendship, the opinions of the peer group can be acceptable criticism. Peers are readily available to act as instant sounding boards for ideas. Moreover, by listening to or reading each others' writing, children can be assisted in their own thinking. Looking at the writing of others provides a model that can be used later.

Children learn from each other

Teaching at any level involves many different and time-consuming tasks. It is interesting to build up a list with your class, and discuss which roles might be shared rather than being only the teacher's responsibility. (Most teachers have had the feeling of being 'spread too thin'!)

For discussion

Here is a possible structure for a discussion about how tasks could be shared:

1   In class/in small groups/individually/in journals, discuss the qualities of a good teacher.

2   Build up a list of tasks which the teacher has to perform: provide stimulus, plan lesson timings, look after equipment, buy equipment, keep the register, give advice, mark books, write tests, give tasks.

3   Discuss which tasks need to be done exclusively by the teacher and which could or should be shared.

The following articles show how teachers can help children to become more involved with their own learning, by encouraging them to work collaboratively, to share aims and ideas and to respond to each others' writing. This allows the teacher to stand back and observe the writing process, and gives more opportunity to choose the most helpful and effective points at which to intervene.

This teacher embarked on a series of writing projects which required collaboration with her class of eight- to nine-year-olds.

Working in groups . . .

In terms of organisation and efficient use of teacher time (a constant nightmare with a big class), pupil collaboration made the assessment of the writing less of a problem and much more satisfying. Where two, three of four children were engaged together on the same piece of writing, I was able to offer positive and effective help throughout, rather than marking in the traditional way after the event. There was dialogue between children, so that the writers became involved in the assessment process too.

It's fair to say that children have to *learn* to write collaboratively, and they do get better at it. It must also be stressed that collaborative writing is not the only way to write. Like adults, children sometimes need to be quiet, sometimes silent and maybe even alone.

Julie Addé, Broadway East First School, Newcastle-upon-Tyne

Esyllt Maelor, one of the Gwynedd Writing Project Co-ordinators, summarises her reactions to a collaborative writing environment.

. . . And in pairs

'I'm stuck.'
'Will you help me?'
'This piece isn't good enough. What shall I do now?'

Teachers are very familiar with comments such as these. They can be a problem, especially when they are being voiced in simultaneous confusion from every corner of the classroom. Dealing with a classroom full of children who all require individual attention can be an ordeal for teachers, and they will inevitably feel that they cannot cope adequately, and cannot be everywhere at the same time.

Perhaps there is too much pressure on children to work as if they were in solitary cells with invisible walls separating them from the rest of the class. Their only channel of communication is along the line connecting them with the teacher. Placing more responsibility on the pupils themselves, rather than keeping them dependent on the teacher, not only helps them to develop, but also gives the teacher more time to intervene effectively. Is it not appropriate to build up an atmosphere of co-operation in the classroom so that a child may turn to a friend or partner for assistance? Children can certainly benefit from each others' comments, and I have been surprised to observe how sensitive children can be in their response to each others' work.

Esyllt Maelor, Gwynedd Writing Project Co-ordinator

Some of the schools involved in the Writing Project have, for some time now, encouraged children to work in pairs. What was the children's response to working in this manner? This is an example of a child's response to a piece of written work done by a friend.

The Strange Isle

The wind whistles in the cold
breeze of the night. The sound of
screams haunt the nocturnal animals.
An old tree collapses to the floor with
the angel of death beside it. The birds
pray that the tree that their nest
is in wont collapse and destroy their child.
Bats fly from tree to tree. A
ball of bogies is sitting on the
ground where an owl eats a mouse
but there is no sound in the Strange
Isle.

Very well done. You have portrayed this island very
well. It was a spine chilling experience reading
it, and I felt I was really there watching
the Bats fly. I liked many of your descriptions
for example "The wind whistles in the cold
breeze of the night" and I especially liked
this one "An old tree collapses to the floor with
the angel of death beside it. That sentence
made me see pictures in my mind of this
black angel laughing. I think
you stopped writing at exactly the
right place, and I liked your closing
sentence. The only thing I would watch is
the spelling for example
could
deth
whith. But it didn't effect the enjoyment
of the description at all. Well done

We can underestimate children, not appreciating how capable they are of responding to each others' work in a responsive and constructive manner. If they are given the opportunity to work naturally in this way on a day-to-day basis, they will develop an increasingly sophisticated and mature response. They will gradually develop a similar response to their own work.

How can children become effective response partners?

A five-year-old (or a ten-year-old or a fifteen-year-old) has produced a piece of writing. It is shown to a peer to read. What sort of reaction will occur? Will it be helpful? constructive? sympathetic? positive? It might be. But there again it might not. It is the teacher's responsibility to structure the learning environment so that children do learn to assist each other.

It is easy to underestimate children's capabilities. Even very young children can learn to respond thoughtfully to each others' writing with little overt guidance from the teacher. Being on the receiving end of response from others helps to define for the writer and the reader what sort of response is helpful.

Collaborators

Two Shropshire reception class children, Fiona and Neil, were invited by their teacher, Sheila Hughes, to help each other to write, once a week. Fiona wrote herself and Neil dictated to the teacher. Fiona and Neil also produced pictures to accompany the text. Each week they exchanged their writing, read each other's work, and made comments which the teacher wrote underneath. These are some extracts.

Week 1

Fiona wrote:	*'I like black because I had a toy black dog and I have always wanted a real life black dog.'*
Neil commented:	*'She could have made it better if she'd put legs on the dog.'*
Neil wrote:	*'I like yellow wallpaper and I am going to ask my dad if I can have some.'*
Fiona commented:	*'He should have put "wallpaper" at the end of his story.'*

Week 2

Fiona wrote:	*'Red makes my Mummy happy. She has a red Renault 5 car and there is a lot of room in the boot.'*
Neil commented:	*'She should have put spokes on the wheels and two lights front and back.'*
Neil wrote:	*'This is a red lorry and I like it.'*
Fiona commented:	*'He should have said where the lorry was going and why he liked it.'*

The teacher was, at first, a little discouraged. The children seemed rather negative in their comments and Neil seemed to be concerned only with the drawing. However, they were revealing considerable knowledge about the needs of text and drawings, and they wanted to continue. After six weeks observable changes had occurred.

Week 6

Fiona wrote:	*'The bear is trying to get some honey out of a tree. He looks very cuddly but really he is dangerous.'*
Neil commented:	*'Draw a bigger tree. It is a good story.'*
Neil wrote:	*'My teddy bear is sitting by a tree thinking about doing something naughty.'*
Fiona commented:	*'Ears and paws on the bear. I would like to know what naughty things this teddy was going to do.'*

(These extracts are also discussed in the Theme Pack *Becoming a Writer*.)

It is interesting to see how, even in this short time, both the children's own writing and their responses have developed. The environment provided by the teacher is crucial. Children do not automatically become effective response partners for each other. To a greater or lesser extent the build-up of confidence and expertise has to be stage-managed, but with the aim of eventually removing the supportive framework so that control and responsibility pass to the children.

Sometimes teachers inadvertently give children misleading messages about the features they think important in writing. When children are asked to respond to each others' work, their responses may reflect their teacher's style in an uncomfortable way. Responders need to know whether they are responding to content or surface features, or both, or something else.

This is a response to a second year Secondary pupil's CDT instruction booklet, by a pupil in another second year class.

Jan '88   1 (A)

This is a very neat and tidy project Which has lot's of diagrams and Safety procautions. It is also very Well set out and it is colourful.   Very Good

How can teachers help pupils learn to become effective response partners (and thus critical readers of their own work as well as other people's)? Different teachers have tried different techniques; Roger Whitewick of Oakfield Middle School, Frome, used these sheets.

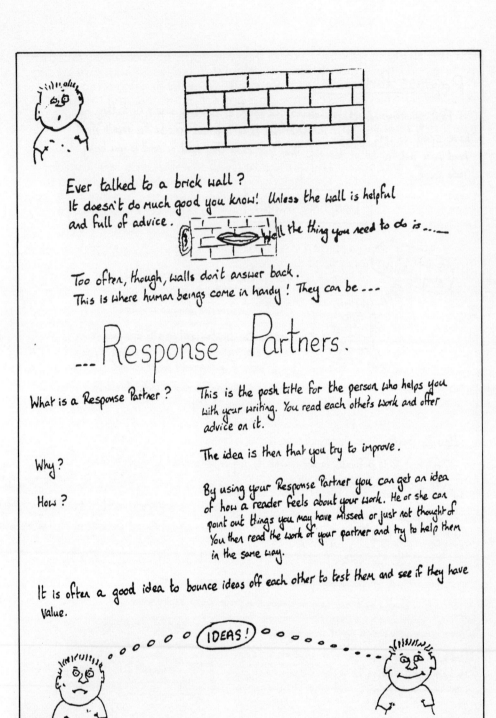

Ever talked to a brick wall?
It doesn't do much good you know! Unless the wall is helpful and full of advice. Well the thing you need to do is ......

Too often, though, walls don't answer back.
This is where human beings come in handy! They can be ...

... Response Partners.

What is a Response Partner? — This is the posh title for the person who helps you with your writing. You read each other's work and offer advice on it.

Why? — The idea is then that you try to improve.

How? — By using your Response Partner you can get an idea of how a reader feels about your work. He or she can point out things you may have missed or just not thought of. You then read the work of your partner and try to help them in the same way.

It is often a good idea to bounce ideas off each other to test them and see if they have value.

IDEAS!

Response Partners 2.

First you remember that whatever you think of somebody else's work they may have spent a long time on it. What you think is drivel may be the result of hard work and a lot of thought. The last thing they want or need is you being rude about it.

> DON'T BE RUDE.

You may not necessarily like what your partner has written but you can be constructive in your criticism.

Constructive criticism is designed to help. Destructive criticism is pulling a piece of writing apart for no reason.

Everything you say or write should be designed to help

How to Start.

At first it is difficult to know what to say or write about somebody else's work. If you follow these steps it will help.

1. Read through the piece of writing.
2. Now read through it again.
3. Find two Golden Lines
4. Think of two good points about the piece of writing.
5. Think about one way in which the piece could be improved.

Make sure you are a good response partner!
Don't let your partner think that he or she is better off talking to a brick wall!

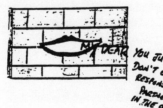

Glenda Walton's class in Hollinswood Middle School, Telford, Shropshire produced 'social worker reports' as a follow-up to a television programme, *Izzy*.

Pupils were then asked to choose a partner with whom they felt comfortable and with whom they would share and try to improve their work. Glenda prepared two sets of cards, the first dealing with the substance and quality of the writing.

Pair work   **CARD ONE**

Choose a partner to work with

Your task   *Partner's task*

Read your work aloud   Listen carefully to
your partner's reading

Both of you

Try and answer the following questions:
1. Do you think the writing is interesting/enjoyable?
2. Is there anything missing in this piece?
3. Is there anything which is not clear or accurate?
4. Can you suggest any helpful words or expressions?
5. Can you suggest a more suitable beginning or ending to the piece?
6. Do you think it is too long or too short?
7. Can anything be missed out?
8. Has the writer written what (s)he was asked to do?
Write down suggested improvements on a separate piece of paper.

Following further discussion, a set of cards dealing with spelling, punctuation and vocabulary was introduced.

Pair work   **CARD TWO**

With your partner, read through your writing again.

Try and answer the following questions:
1. Are there any spelling mistakes? Underline them in pencil.
2. Check the punctuation. Are the full stops and capital letters in the right places? Correct them in pencil.
3. Show, on your writing, where you wish to make alterations.
4. Ask the teacher at this point if you feel you need more help.
5. Write out your revised version.

Responding: some guidelines

Which section of the piece was most successful? Why?

Which section was the least successful? Why?

Is there any way the beginning might have been made more gripping?

Is it a good ending? Might it be improved? How?

Are there any sections which do not seem to fit in?

Are there any parts of the piece, people in it, etc. which might be more fully developed?

Are there any sections you did not understand?

Are there phrases/sentences where the expression might be varied more? Where the vocabulary might be enriched?

Did you spot any errors of grammar, punctuation, paragraphing, spelling, use of slang..? Gently point these out.

Did you enjoy the piece? Why? Why not?

This sheet was designed by Gill Fox, the Cheshire Writing Project Co-ordinator, for use with fourteen- and fifteen-year-olds.

Response partners in Gymnastics

During 1984/85 I was involved in a DES Joint Regional Course 'The role of Physical Education in the whole curriculum'. I became interested in the teaching of Gymnastics through a reciprocal teaching style which emphasises social development. At about the same time I became involved in the use of 'think books' through my involvement with OCEA (Oxford Certificate of Educational Achievement). The think books were used as part of the school's tutorial system and had been developed through the work of teachers who were part of the Somerset and Wiltshire Write to Learn Project.

By September 1986 I felt confident enough to combine these two strands of thought during an eight-week block of work in Gymnastics with a group of twelve-year-old boys.

The established format for Gymnastics involved a work booklet containing more than ninety elements. When an activity was performed correctly by a pupil and passed by the pupil's partner, this was recorded on a record sheet. I decided to add another piece of paper — the 'think sheet'.

During the first session, we discussed the sheets and talked about the value of recording success in one lesson as a springboard for the next. The children therefore became familiar and confident with the framework.

Subsequent lessons followed this format:

1   Place apparatus in position.

2   Receive and read individual think sheets.

3   Receive work booklet and record sheet.

4   Choose a partner (if not already paired).

5   Decide which activities to perform until ten minutes before end of lesson.

6   Write about partner. (During this, teacher starts packing away apparatus.)

7   Read individual think sheets.

8   Return work booklet, record sheet and think sheet.

9   Pack away apparatus.

10   Teacher reads and comments, if necessary, on think sheets.

Writing about each other's work can have benefits in all subject areas where thinking about one's own performance is important. In Brian Baker's PE lessons, students helped each other to look at their development.

No one lost their sheets, but in general, using sheets resulted in less writing than I had previously observed in notebooks. Maybe this was because of the single sheets, or maybe it was the nature of the activity.

At the end of the block of work I asked the pupils for their comments on having to write about their partner. These are some of their replies:

'Good because I could express myself better.'
'A good idea because you could say things which you would not want other people to see.'
'I liked writing about my partner because I could be truthful.'
'Grown up.'

The following comments indicate what the pupils thought about reading about themselves:

'Interesting to find out what I was like.'
'All right because if it said you don't try hard enough you can try harder the next day.'
'Fun because you knew what he really thought of you.'
'Very good because I could find out how good I was.'

The atmosphere in these lessons is different from that in previous sessions. I feel the pupils have become more involved in the process of comparing, contrasting, drawing conclusions and communicating through the use of response partners.

Finally, their responses have made me more aware that pupils are quite capable of making astute, accurate and helpful written comments not only about an activity but also about their peers. Many other teachers involved in the Project have found the same thing.

Brian Baker, Oakfield Middle School, Frome, Somerset

Means to an end

I wanted to achieve a better understanding of the writing process; the focus was on the early stages of writing. I hoped that the pupils would also begin to feel part of a supportive writing community. Written comments from other pupil-writers and any consequent consultation would provide the means to these ends; short story writing would be the vehicle.

A wide range of short stories was made available. During three forty-five minute lessons over three weeks, fourth year pupils individually read as many short stories as possible, noticing the writers' techniques, especially in the opening sentences. Small friendship groups fed into a whole class discussion on different genres (for example, war stories or romance), noting the characteristics of different types of story. Each pupil then chose a type of story to write. Thus, a whole class would be writing narrative, but within that loose framework individual choice was to be paramount. Pupils who had chosen the same genre then formed a group, and discussion focused on the possibilities, limitations and requirements indicated by the chosen genre.

At home, each pupil wrote the beginning of a story, using double spacing so that other pupils could read it and offer written comments on it. As many other pupils as possible read each text and jotted down constructive, signed comments. The reader-critics would comment on each others' observations, and each storywriter had a right of reply to the critics. Examples from those first drafts demonstrate the pupils' involvement in this work.

It is sometimes helpful to focus on a particular aspect of writing. Certainly, specific responses are often more helpful than general ones. Bernadette Fitzgerald from Avon was interested in the early stages of story writing — the first jottings that develop into a finished narrative, in particular the story beginnings. Pupils received comments from a variety of response partners.

Makes me want to throw up →

"Hello Sexy Give us a kiss" Tom Shouted.

Makes me want to read it!

There was no reply from the shy Girl called Sharon.

Sounds like Tom is getting a bit pushy.

who had just moved into the town ...

very good descriptive words, it sounds like
something straight from a book Not my kind of
story.

It's really creepy - mysterious, very interesting

What next? I want to read more

Boys Boys Boys don't you ever write for girls although
saying that the description is very very good but you
can tell a boy has written it because there is no
words for girls.

Each storywriter had to choose whether to adopt some, all or none of the suggestions and criticisms offered. A few pupils rejected their first ideas completely and started again — I stressed that all writers do this; some pupils elected to make minor changes or to include more details; the work of a happy minority had been so well received that no changes were deemed necessary.

I was pleased that after three forty-five minute lessons spent reading published short stories, two more lessons devoted to discussing genre and narrative techniques, and one further lesson of reading and commenting on each others' work, the majority of children were ready to write the second draft of an effective opening to a story.

Through active involvement in the writing process, these pupils had:

- become aware of the first stage of the writing process

- become aware of each other as writers — some of the isolation of writers had been broken down

- been shown by peers some of the strengths/weaknesses of their own writing and, most importantly, had been shown how to improve it

- experienced a shift in classroom power as the constructive criticism had come from their peers and not from the teacher

- experienced the joys and hardships of writing for an audience

As readers and critics, the pupils took seriously the demanding task of reflecting on other pupils' writing in progress and offering constructive criticism. As creative writers, they anxiously awaited the return of their work, eager to see what the audience had thought of it.

Bernadette Fitzgerald, Hengrove School, Bristol, Avon

Teachers' comments

'I tried getting the children to read each others' work and give oral comments. As the children were so unused to doing this their comments were very superficial but I hope, with more practice, these will develop.'

If your pupils have tried collaborative writing, you might design a questionnaire to gauge their response. The following are examples of answers from Tony Hickling's class in Dalton Middle School in Ratingen, Germany (SCEA) after working collaboratively on poems about a special place in their memories.

'I get more ideas to help me with my writing.'

'My partner has helped me with the organisation of my ideas.'

'My partner has helped me think more deeply about my ideas.'

'It gives me an insight into what other people think and might think about my writing.'

'It helps you to see some or all of your faults.'

'It helped me learn how to criticise and be criticised without hurt feelings and guilt.'

'Your partner can appreciate how you feel and what you are trying to say more than a teacher.'

'It taught me how other people think and how they transfer their thoughts on to paper.'

'I like to have advice from someone my own age.'

'No teacher help was needed. He left us to our own devices, which taught us more than spoon feeding.'

'I feel we can teach each other certain things just as well as a teacher.'

'I feel more in control of what I write.'

'I didn't get much help from my partner.'

'My partner was too concerned with her own work and wasn't bothered about mine.'

'All her comments were about things that were wrong.'

Teachers' comments

'. . . The next piece of writing I chose was a report which we wrote after a class visit to the local radio station. We basically kept the same working pairs as before. The children each produced an individual written account and then exchanged their reports. They seemed to organise themselves well at this point, waiting for each other to finish writing before asking for an idea, opinion or word to help with their own work. The noise level in the class was not over the limit but they obviously did need to talk to each other at various times. I was so pleased with the reports that I decided to allow them to rewrite their reports on the computer. (This process takes time.) Now we plan to photocopy the print-outs and make a class book to be shown to the radio station team and then kept in school. The original computer sheets may then go home.'

'. . . The resulting pieces of work were of a better standard than usual, although the content was derivative (eg UFOs, the Vietnam war, ghosts, football, horses). The second year class reacted in a responsible way to the workshop approach which was pleasing. The discussions were relevant and critical and the pupils were able to share their problems.'

'I adopted this collaborative process with a fourth year class who were working on short stories for their GCSE course . . . The pupils benefited from having their writing discussed during the creative process and having an immediate audience response. The final short stories reflected this stimulus to rewriting and editing, providing in some cases the best pieces of work during the course. (One boy, a science fiction buff, wrote seventeen pages; previously his assignments had tended to be brief.) However, some of the stories tended to be derivative. I did wonder if the focus on genre and structure, together with an audience of peers whose expectations were similar to their own, had meant that individuals had kept to conventional approaches.'

For discussion

Much has been said of the need to encourage children's sense of ownership of their writing, valuing their ideas and points of view rather than always measuring their work against an adult model and finding it wanting. But can the process go too far? At what stage (and how) should the teacher intervene to wean the writer off the seventh all-action adventure or the little pony waiting patiently for its rider to return?

3 Response from others

The value of using an accessible audience for writing in school has been emphasised again and again. Writing for real audiences was the theme for two of the LEAs in the National Writing Project and this approach has permeated the work of all the others. One of the Theme Packs in this series is exclusively about the issues raised by writing for real audiences; the subject is also touched on here.

An audience can be yet another source of feedback, allowing writers to gauge the success of their efforts. If the audience is accessible and feedback occurs during the writing of a piece, the writer can take account of audience reaction and develop the writing accordingly. If feedback occurs at the end, the writer can accommodate audience reaction in future writing.

Writing for others is an opportunity for the community of writers and readers referred to in the last section to broaden, to include other classrooms, other schools, parents, family and friends, the local community, local industry and the media. The benefits are reciprocal; the emerging writer receives feedback, and the surrounding community begins to work with and understand some of the things that the writer, the class and the school are trying to do.

Outside agencies can provide stimulus as well as response. There are many instances of interaction with, for example, older people in sheltered housing who have provided first-hand insights into Britain in the 1930s for eager young historians; with classes in other towns and other countries to give a new understanding of the different environments in which people live. Correspondence can be by letter, postcard or electronic mail. It is important to remember that there is a surprisingly accessible world outside the classroom door. There is room here for only a brief selection of ideas with a bias towards the response that the writers receive.

Feedback from younger readers

Throughout the Project and elsewhere, probably the most popular audience for children's writing is younger children, usually in the same school or a feeder school. Younger children provide a demanding but not threatening readership, who must be listened to in matters of taste and preference.

Books with a difference

Last summer, my fourth year Juniors wrote storybooks for the Infants — an experience which we all found exciting. This sparked off a desire to continue the liaison with the younger children. So, in September, with a different set of fourth years, we began our year's work with a 'getting to know you' theme.

I gave the children a skeleton topic web with *'Me'* at the centre. After a lot of discussion, they filled it in. Using the web, they put together a folder of work about themselves to take with them to the Infant school. During the visit I was superfluous! The children disappeared into odd corners and had a wonderful time getting to know each other with the help of the work they had done.

This was the preparation for a joint trip to the woods, where the children worked with their partners from the Infant school all day. Each pair had a nature trail booklet, and my children industriously looked for the trail markers and pointed out the relevant areas of interest to their partners.

In the afternoon, the children had the opportunity to follow up their own interests: looking for mini-beasts, finding objects with particular attributes like 'rough' or 'smooth', collecting leaves or bits of bark.

Story writing is not the only possible activity. Gail Mould's fourth year Junior class in Basingstoke wrote information books for Infants while Aileen Madders' class combined story writing for Infants in the same school with visits from professional writers. In both cases, the audience provided response for the writers to gauge their own success and develop their work.

I had discussed follow-up activities with the Infant teacher, and on our return we asked the children to choose something they had found to study in detail. These 'finds' included bits of old wood, one complete with a family of woodlice, a skull, and various other interesting things. We made a class storybook of the work, and took it to the Infant school when we went to see their follow-up work.

I wanted my class to write an information book next. This proved much harder than writing storybooks. I asked them to base their books on areas of work which had some connection with our trip to the woods, and all the ideas were at least loosely connected with natural history. They worked singly or in pairs as they chose.

The book was to be presented to the Infant library, so I asked them to think particularly about the needs of younger children. First they went to the Infant school to look at their books and talk to the children about which ones they liked best and why. Then they gathered together all the resources they would need.

I have always found it difficult, if not impossible, to stop children regurgitating chunks of text books in their own topic work; this was an attempt to do just that. I was particularly keen for them to think beyond books: to collect pictures; to talk to people with subject knowledge; to look at slides of the real thing wherever possible.

This time the children made their own topic plans using a similar strategy to the *'Me'* topic web. I drew up a chart of suggestions for each piece of work — thinking, making notes, drafting, discussing and doing a final copy. Then they were ready to begin writing.

Having produced some final drafts they set off to the Infant school and my fears were confirmed. They came back in a state of great agitation — the Infants couldn't understand what they had written. What were they going to do about it? Storybooks had relied on imagination and lively writing; in the information books we needed to be technically accurate with facts and drawings, while making sure the information was accessible.

We sat down together to chat. I told the children that I felt we'd reached crisis point and asked what, if anything, they thought could be done. Should we continue? The children were far more positive than I was. Yes, they wanted to produce their books. Together we drew up another sheet of helpful suggestions. It was decided that:

- the books must be colourful

- half writing and half picture is the best layout

- big complicated words are not appropriate

- we must use words the children are familiar with

- we must not use long sentences

- pictures must be accurate

- a glossary would help; it could be called 'Words you might not know'

- a contents page is needed

- an introduction would help

The children also decided that their books must offer something different from the content of most information books. They could include board games, quizzes, crosswords, cartoons, word searches and various puzzles.

One girl had a hidden duck on each page for the younger child to find, and little comments throughout. A couple of boys had a small picture on the corner of each page, to 'animate' by flicking the pages. They were beginning to realise that they had to think for themselves and not just use other reference books. They began to appreciate that because they were children too, they could offer an understanding that adults could not.

They became quite critical of some existing reference books. They realised that often the pictures and the writing were not on the same level, and that sometimes books appeared patronising. They knew that their own illustrations might not have been brilliant, but they decided that books in the library often left a lot to be desired too. This was a valuable lesson for them.

What WILL happen next?!

You now have a choice of 8 different endings.

READ ON . . . . .

Ending 6.

TREASURE

Janet and matthew and the imps started diging they where detrmend not to give up then they hit something hard but it was just a rock after two hours they gave up for the night. The next day was just the same they dug and they dug untill there arms aked but they kept on going. The next day they had a meeting they studied the map utill there eyes aked and for the rest of the day. They had tied every were exepet under a big rock. The next day they rolled it away they saw a rusty old box the imps ran to get it they shouted "ITS THE TREASURE" they opened it with a grinding noise it was full of gold coins. Then janet saw a white button she pressed it the ceiling opened and a ladder and they climed out and they forgot every thing. And the imps were forgoten aswell. .THE END.

The map

Having written the book to their satisfaction and, equally importantly, to the satisfaction of the Infant children, they sequenced the work and numbered the pages. Then we discussed the need for a contents page, an index, a glossary and an introduction. Again they looked at existing books to see the layout, and compared the merits of different approaches. Sorting out the glossary was challenging and required a lot of work. Deciding which words to include, sequencing the words, and then writing good definitions — it wasn't easy. It resulted in much head-scratching, mine included.

Finally, the children made the books. Some were so carried away with their work that they made three books out of the material they had collected. Pleased with the results, they felt it had been worth the effort. It certainly made them think carefully about the purpose and requirements of reference books, and I think they will be more critical of books in future.

Gail Mould, Kempshott Junior School, Basingstoke, Hampshire

A community of writers in my classroom

My interest in the National Writing Project followed two introductory meetings with staff from other local schools who were becoming involved in the Project. A colleague and I left the meetings with a commitment to involve the sixty top Junior children whom we taught in writing stories for younger children. At this stage we decided that the audience should be the Lower School children in our own school.

We needed a suitable starting point. At the time, there was some publicity about a new local author called James Driscoll, who was about to launch a series of storybooks for young children called *The Shoe People*. These were a group of imaginary characters based on an amazing variety of shoes.

Venture, a BBC documentary series, devoted a full programme to James Driscoll and the evolution of his shoe characters, and this was shown to the fourth year children. There followed a great deal of excited discussion, especially when we explored the possibility of inviting James Driscoll into school. Despite his heavy business programme, he accepted our invitation at incredibly short notice.

The afternoon was a great success; it really fired the children's imagination. James Driscoll was questioned endlessly about his characters and their origins, and he showed a video of the various stages in the production of an animated cartoon of one of his stories. (This was later shown on television.) The video included the use of 'storyboards', a technique which the children were to use themselves in the development of their own stories.

The children gradually found out for themselves the difficulties they were likely to face in the weeks ahead: the time involved; the amount of work that is rejected and has to be rewritten; the dogged perseverance needed to complete a story.

The children were encouraged to bring into school a wide range of books which they themselves had enjoyed, or which younger brothers and sisters were still enjoying. Series like the *Mr. Men* stories and *The Vegetable People* proved to be the most popular and prolific. We built up a huge display of these books which were read avidly and studied in terms of layout, illustration, simplicity of language, storyline, content and appeal.

Small groups then visited some of the Lower School classes and questioned the children about the story features they particularly liked. Their answers included such things as *'exciting adventures'*, *'witches'*, *'ghosts'*, *'animals'*, *'funny bits'*, *'good pictures'* and, most evident of all, *'happy endings'*. The discussion here was most rewarding. It was not directed in any way, and the spontaneity of the younger children overcame the nervous questioning of the older ones. We wished we had taped some of these sessions.

We now felt we could make a start, and after more discussion the children decided that they needed to create their characters before tackling the storyline. Each child developed his/her own family of characters. They made drawings and then built up short character studies of each, showing their personalities, lifestyles, habits and foibles.

We then felt we needed to share and exchange ideas more easily, so each child did an enlarged illustration of his/her favourite character with accompanying notes. These were built into a large wall display for easier viewing and discussion; it was also a visual introduction to such original characters as Adam Aerosol, Grandma MacBrolly, Belle Belle and Willie Worm (to name but a few)!

The next stage was to plan the actual story, and for this we used storyboards depicting the main points of the story with a series of rapid illustrations. The storyboards were exchanged and read amongst the class, and any criticism and advice were worked upon, if the writer agreed! Once the storyboards were completed the children developed each part of the board as a page of their book. This was done in rough, and each page was discussed and corrected, if necessary, with each child individually.

Once the rough drafts were completed, the writers returned to the Lower School classes and read their stores aloud to see what the response was at this stage. Was the storyline clear? Had the characters emerged successfully? They also read each others' rough drafts, and any changes deemed necessary were made, before they went on to the next draft.

The children enjoyed this stage of the project and took a great deal of pride in their presentation, after giving careful thought to their choice of book size, layout and position of illustrations in relation to the text. It did, however, prove to be somewhat laborious and time-consuming, as no one wanted to rush it.

Generally, the children opted to work on a page at a time, preparing text and illustration together. A few chose to complete all the writing before starting the illustrations. The illustrations were detailed and meticulous, and at this stage the children were encouraged to take their folders home to complete the artwork.

Finally the front covers were designed, and then the books were bound and added to the growing 'library' in the classroom. The children were eager to complete their books and to read each others', and were rightly most complimentary about all the finished products.

The stories were now ready for an audience, and an arrangement was made with staff in the Lower School to set aside the last half hour of each morning for a full half term. During this time, each child in turn took his/her book to one of the Lower School classes and read it to the whole class. The writers were rather hesitant and nervous on departure, but returned to the classroom delighted with their reception. This special storytime was eagerly awaited each day by reader and listener alike, and was so exciting and encouraging after all the hard work. It proved, in so many different ways, to be the most valuable part of the project, and was enhanced by the support given by the Lower School class teachers. They guided the discussion on the individual stories, and the younger children contributed in their usual astute and honest way! The class teachers also made short but useful written comments (for my reference) on each story's oral presentation. This was the part of the project from which I excluded myself, as I thought the readers needed to feel that they could do it on their own.

Another spin-off from this exchange was that the Lower School children besieged their class teacher with requests to write their own stories. They in turn came and read them to my children who were equally responsive and enthusiastic, and often surprised by the high standard of their efforts.

The project as a whole ran for two terms, and this was considerably longer than I had envisaged. Time allocation during the first term had to be all-embracing, and after that we decided to work to a 'completion date' when any spare moment the children had could be voluntarily taken up with their books. The children gained enormously from being involved in this project, it gave their writing a real purpose, and their enthusiasm rarely wavered.

Aileen Madders, Tenterfields Primary School, Dudley

<u>Fred Fireman</u>

Fred Fireman was very jolly and always shared his things with other people. If any one wanted something doing he would do it for them. Every one was his friend except for Mark milkman. Fred's best friend was Florence Fire engine who he worked with and shared his house with. Fred always liked getting up in the morning and bouncing off to work with some of his friends.

David
Maydew.

FRED FIREMAN.

For discussion

Discuss with your class the range of people to whom they write or could write.

What effect are they trying to make in their writing?

What sort of response do they want?

What sort of response do they receive?

What effect do the responses have on them?

Would the answers be different for you/their parents/friends/ famous people?

Feedback from other children and adults

'The Blow-away Kite'

'The Blow-away Kite' was the result of an experiment in collaborative writing between my class of seven- and eight-year-olds at Benton Park Primary School and Julie Addé's of eight- and nine-year-olds at Broadway East First School, with each class writing alternate chapters of a book. Collaboration also occurred within each class, as children worked in groups at the computer using the Quinkey microwriters.

In my class, every child wrote his/her own initial version of Chapter One, but four children, two boys and two girls, worked together using Quinkey. This made it easier for them to read each others' writing and to edit their work. When they had finished writing they illustrated their work, placed the chapter in a large brown envelope and sent it to Broadway East. The class eagerly awaited the response, and were very excited when a package arrived a week later. I read their chapter to them again to remind them of the story and then continued with Chapter Two (written by Broadway East children). They listened with interest and were keen to see the illustration.

They noticed that the last sentence of the new chapter was in capital letters and ended with a question mark. We discussed the need to leave the readers wondering what was going to happen next. I was interested to see that many of the children used this device in their next instalment.

Chapters Three and Five were written by two more groups of children, two boys and two girls in each case. They found it a more difficult task than the first group, because as well as containing something new and exciting, each successive chapter had to relate to what had gone before.

Julie's class wrote the final chapter and made 'The Blow-away Kite' into a lovely book with a choice of eight different endings. My children had great fun reading them and discussing which ending they preferred and why.

For the Summer Term, Julie and I chose to look at certain aspects of a story in detail. Julie's class would draw and write about a house (in the widest sense of the word — a place where someone or something could live). My class would then write about who lived there.

In preparation for this, I divided my class into mixed ability groups of four or five children and, after discussions, they wrote about a house. At the end of the afternoon, I asked the children to take a printed copy of their group's description and to ask someone at home to help them write about who lived in the house. We had previously asked parents and a grandparent to contribute to our class books, but this was the first time I had asked them to write in collaboration with their child.

The children generally worked with one parent but in some cases the whole family worked together. One girl wrote with her fifteen-year-old babysitter. A boy whose group had described two houses — a lopsided one and a haunted one — informed me that *My work has two words that I bet even you don't know the meaning of*'. He described how he and his father had looked things up in his father's very big books. For the inhabitants of the haunted house they had chosen the name Eldritch because it meant *'unearthly'* and for those in the lopsided house the name Juggins meaning *'someone rather silly'*. One girl and her parents gave the inhabitants of their haunted house very appropriate names such as Sir Sebastian Severed-Head, Lady Gloriana Ghoul, Doctor Mortimer Mortuary and identical twins Shiver and Shriek Severed-Head.

In the first of the following examples, parents and other children were involved as helpers in a collaborative activity between two Primary classes. In the second, parents acted as collaborators and correspondents. The third describes response from an adult author.

A couple of weeks later, eleven brown envelopes arrived from Julie's class containing lovely bright pictures and descriptions of a range of houses including a 'desert house', a 'little big house', a 'clock house' and a 'wibbly wobbly house'. I grouped the children, and after a brief discussion each group was given a brown envelope and asked to describe who or what might live in the house shown inside.

The clock house

The clock people were Happy. The clock People never stopped ticking, The CLOCK People's face's were like round heads, and the man clock had a musstash. Which was drawn on and his eye's were open and when they go to bed their eye's never close. Sussy clock loved her skirt

Mamy clock   Dady clock   sister clock   baby clock.

The clock people

For some of the children it was a very difficult task and several of them found that it helped to draw pictures of the people or creatures first and then write about them. It was fascinating to see how carefully they studied what Julie's children had written and drawn. Demanding though this activity was, many of the children really seemed to enjoy it once they got started. The next morning I was greeted with cries of *'When can we have the brown envelopes again?'*

One girl who finds it hard to write things down was writing about the wobbly cat who lived in the wobbly house, using wobbly writing. She asked me how to write *'spaghetti'* because the cat's whiskers were like spaghetti. I said, *'Oh, you mean they were sticking out straight'*, to which she indignantly replied, *'No, cooked spaghetti because it's wobbly.'*

I had joined my class in January and the Writing Project a few weeks later. As an inexperienced teacher of children of this age group trying to produce examples in a short period of time for a Writing Project workshop, I certainly made mistakes. However, when I felt that things were going badly, the children would often write something or make some comment which made it seem worthwhile. I learned a lot and I think the children did too. Writing can be a very frustrating exercise and it is certainly hard work, but it can be a rewarding and enjoyable experience — especially when it is shared.

Sue Cross, Benton Park Primary School, Newcastle-upon-Tyne

The practice of involving parents has many advantages. They can provide help with the writing; they can form an accessible readership; they can also learn about what is really going on in classrooms. Lesley Crowe had just completed her probationary year and was interested, having joined the Croydon Project, in involving parents. As the parents helped the children in their writing, their perception of the writing curriculum changed as did the children's attitude to their own and each others' writing.

Writing partners

I was teaching a class of thirty-five first year Juniors. They were a lively bunch who contributed positively to most tasks.

I wanted to involve parents but was not sure how to do it. Looking back, I now realise that the main reason for this was my lack of confidence in using parents in the classroom. Then I was approached by two mothers expressing a willingness to help. This actually arose from an informal chat about the size of the class and how this concerned them as parents. I accepted their offer gladly, and after talking about the Project and what we were trying to do, I involved them in a programme of work which concentrated initially on imaginative writing.

Mrs. Hill and Mrs. Dean-Osgood came into school one morning a week and worked together with different groups of eight or nine children. At first they relied totally upon me to provide them with the subjects for writing and these were linked with whatever topic we were following at the time. As their confidence grew they began to suggest their own ideas for discussion and writing. Many an hour was spent, by the mothers, in the school library and even the local library searching for material to provide stimuli for the group. My role changed from instigator, through working partner and eventually to onlooker.

The mothers' attitude to the children's learning experience changed noticeably as the work developed. In the beginning they accepted, without question, any writing ideas offered by the children. Even if they were aware that a certain child had given them a piece of writing which was below their expectation for that child they didn't feel in a position to voice their opinions. Later, the mothers began to encourage the children, through discussion, to develop their ideas. They would ask open-ended questions, suggest ideas themselves and scribe for those children who found difficulty in putting pen to paper but who took great delight in watching their story or poem taking shape. These sessions culminated in the making of books for the reception class. Each person in the group chose a younger child and wrote a book for him/her, after negotiating the content. In about half a term one group of ten children and the two parents wrote, illustrated, laminated and bound the books. The results were a credit to all of them.

The children have gained a great deal through working with the parents. They are more aware of the kinds of support they need and are more positive and constructive in making use of the help adults can give. They have realised the value of interaction with an adult and how this helps them to organise their thoughts, so making the task of writing easier.

Most of the children in my class are now more willing to sit down and talk about their ideas and to make use of advice and criticism. From this, the children have found that there is value in discussing and exchanging ideas on a topic with their peers. I often find a little group pooling suggestions and creating an excellent story. Recently I encouraged Kevin and Kim to read and evaluate each others' work. The result was very surprising and pleasing. I was intrigued to discover that children of this age were actually capable of accepting another child's criticism. They each made positive contributions to their partner's work.

Apart from an increasing understanding of the job of writing, the children are learning about how others read and respond to their writing. It seems to me that they are also engaged in social learning.

The project in my classroom, to date, has proved to be a valuable and enjoyable learning experience for the children, for their parents — and for me.

Lesley Crowe, Smitham Primary School, Coulsdon, Croydon

An author replies

The hungry giant

'One day when Classes 2 and 3 were sitting in the hall for wet playtime the hungry giant on the wall screamed, "I want some milk" without saying please. We all said, "I beg your pardon, without saying please! You really need some manners."

But . . . we all said, "All right, we'll get you some milk."
The hungry giant said, "Milk, I don't want milk, I want milk, honey, bread and butter."

We said, "We cannot give you all that." Rudely, the hungry giant said, "I told you I want some milk, honey, bread and butter."

Then Mr. Jefferson came in and said to the hungry giant, "What on earth are you doing here?"

The giant said for the third time, "I want some food."
Mr. Jefferson said, "Are you joking, this is a school not a restaurant," and banged the giant on the head with his brush.

He fell to the ground and we all laughed with joy.
Mrs. Sutton was so proud of us that she told us we were all going to have a party. All the other children gave us five cheers and we all lived happily ever after without the hungry giant.'

Wayne Creed, Neil Claffey

Response from June Counsel:

Jean Baker invited author June Counsel to work with a class of six-and seven-year-olds in Mountfield Infant School, North Kenton, Newcastle-upon-Tyne. The fruits of their collaboration were a whole range of stories completed within a day and sent off to June Counsel for comment. Two of the pieces and June Counsel's responses are included here.

> The best part of this story is the two main characters, the rude, greedy Hungry Giant and brave, firm, quick acting Mr Jefferson. I believed in them both. They "came off the page" as editors say, and that means you've got their speech and behaviour exactly right.
> So well done! Clever you! I also like the burst of joy in the last paragraph, which leaves the reader as happy as you   June Counsel

James and Jappy

'One day a little boy called James got lost in the forest and he cried and cried and then he screamed as loud as he could but no one heard him.

The little boy saw two girls and the girls said, "Why are you crying?" James was frightened and he ran away. Then he got even more lost.

James met a big dog and the dog was friendly. The dog was called Jappy. James said to

Jappy, *"I saw two girls and I was frightened because I thought they were going to take me away. Please will you help me to find my home?"*

"I will," said Jappy.
"Thank you," said James. Jappy lay down and James got on his back. Jappy took him home.

James' mammy said, "Thank you very much" and gave Jappy some dog food.'

Amit Bahanda, Paul Cummings, Scott Hill

Response fron June Counsel:

This is a lovely little story. Although it is so short, it has everything in it. Fear, running away. sadness, then help, and help from an unexpected character, a friendly dog, and finally a safe happy ending and a reward for the good dog. It is satisfying as it stands but if you were to re-write it, you might like to bring the two girls in and let them explain that they weren't going to hurt James, perhaps say what they were doing in the forest.

June Counsel

4 Becoming a self-critical writer

Whilst writing this, all sorts of ideas are going through my head. Will they like it? Is it too chatty? Does it sound academic enough? Does it appear patronising? What is the nature of the audience? What am I trying to achieve?

I make decisions based on reactions and responses I have received in the past. I have a voice in my head which suggests where I might be writing something inappropriate. Where does this voice come from? With my own writing it has arrived through the painful process of receiving feedback from colleagues and from the effect (or lack of it) that the writing has had in the past. I am motivated because the task is one I care about.

The development of this inner dialogue, this process of self-evaluation, is a goal of much of what we do in school. Writers need opportunities to reflect on their own writing and learning, and on their own development as writers. The articles and accounts which follow demonstrate a range of opportunities which teachers have provided; the strategies which they have made available and which the writers have adapted or further developed for themselves; and their effect.

Journals, think books and learning logs

Some children get caught on a treadmill of producing writing to the teacher's prescription and receiving the teacher's analysis of its success. In these circumstances, the vital learning process of reflection may not happen. One way out of this situation is to remind children that they can write for themselves at their own instigation for their own purposes.

Journals are books that are used to write things down — ideas, jottings, questions — without the writing being criticised or assessed or corrected by someone else. What journals have in common is that they offer writers the opportunity to explore their thoughts and feelings; to consider and comment on their writing and learning experiences; to think on paper about the writing they are doing; to see for themselves their own development. They provide one means of establishing a constructive and sympathetic dialogue between the teacher and the pupil writers.

There is great variation in the ways in which journals have been introduced and used in various writing classrooms. In some cases, the writers themselves have adapted the journal to meet their own needs. Common to all, though, is the new status given to the pupils as learners.

What's in a journal?

Fraction

I don't like Fraction because
I don't under stand fraction
I can do it if there is a picture
with the question but cant if
they is not a picture I look at it
and said I can do it and my
mind goes blank but I was doing the
materal I like very much doing
Scottish primary mathematics
Group Green books.

Vanessa - aged 9

I dont think it is fair that over here in
Britain we have got loads of food
while over in Ethyopia people are
starving to death I reckon that if our
class did a sponsered walk or something
we could raise quite a lot of
money. Also we could make something
to sell people might want to buy
our goods. I mean like badges

Claire - aged 10

Vanessa and Claire use their learning logs to explore difficult concepts and to plan for future action. Such logs can be useful for both the child and the teacher.

After a Science lesson, Simon was asked to jot down what he was learning about and to describe how he felt about the lesson.

veg
fruit
food
sorting
Tv Program
working in
groups
lens
drawing
fun
cut them up
sliced
coulers
in between
sweet and
sour
shape

My Feelings

This morning lesson was good.
I worked in a group with Mark
Darren, Paul, Stuart, Ben.
We got on well, but then
Stuart or Ben began to chatter
about swimming or polteghiste so
the coversation went on for little
while and then stopped so
we were able to work
quietly. Most of the class were
talking about there work
~~or dolls, prams or care bears~~
other from that we worked
quite well. In the end, we
had to make a decision,
who's work would go on
display. Both of mine went on

The teacher also kept a log about the same lesson. Her own evaluation and the comments of the pupils have helped her to identify teaching points and to plan future lessons.

'Many rushed in to do their drawing and weren't prepared to spend the time to study in more detail. A few tried again. Labelling spoiled some of the work. It didn't go as well as at other times — we had prepared by doing set work before. Perhaps I should have done a more formal and structured introduction. I feel I need to read the logs to know how the class felt.'

Think books can be used at any time and for any purpose: from reflective or imaginative writing to reports and experiments with writing.

<u>Shadows</u>

Shadows come nearly all the
time,
Shadows of lights, and
curtains.
Sometimes ones of mine

Angela - aged 10

The teacher's response to journal writing needs to draw the child into a written dialogue:

What I would like to know if possible
is why you think I'm going to get
cross with you over silly things?
Am I a cross person?

I think you will
get cross because I
loose my things and get
tomatoe all over a library
book. I'm sorry I get
so worried all the time

If things are an accident I really
don't and won't get cross.
Don't worry ok!

OK and thats
a deal a DEAL

We have found that journal writing is most successful when:

- teachers respond to the meaning of the journal entry rather than the form

- judgemental responses are avoided

- the questions which are asked reflect the teacher's understanding of what is written

- confidentiality is respected and, thus, trust is established between teacher and child

The success of the logs is reflected in children's comments:

'When I write about things I don't know much about, I learn from what you write, I also get very good advice, sometimes. If I did not have a Think Book I would probably go nuts trying to keep the things I have written to myself.'

'I think it is a brilliant invention and if I am a teacher when I am old, I would probably do this to my pupils.'

Carole Mason and Maisie Foster, Somerset Writing Project Co-ordinators

Point taken

I wanted to improve my teaching so I decided I would try the idea of a work log. It would be a log in which pupils could record their experience of each English lesson: the work done during the lesson and the work which was set afterwards. It would be an account of successes and problems, and would record responses to the lesson. I would reply in writing to the comments, where appropriate.

Most of the pupils responded eagerly to the notion of taking a more active role in what went on in the classroom, although not all the class were prepared to write a responsive log. This was their choice and I respected it.

Louise was apprehensive to start with:

'A worklog is a good idea, but I feel that if I write something about you, you will be cross, or it will sound rude.'

My reply:

'Trust me. I need to have instructive criticism like anybody else.'

They commented on the structure of the lesson:

'There wasn't enough time between each poem to write down your views on them. Robin.'

My reply:

'Point taken — I'll give longer.'

My performance as teacher was sometimes seen to impede the working process:

'I think in some lessons Miss Stacey you talk too much instead of letting us get on with the work. Tracey K.'

My reply:

'Point taken! It's always been my problem.'

'I found the homework quite hard as I didn't really understand what we were supposed to do . . .'

My reply:

'My fault, I'm afraid.'

If the pupils are more involved in their own learning they are naturally going to be appreciative if teachers allow themselves to be influenced by them.

Pupils can tell you in confidence about their needs as learners and about what they enjoy.

'We read for the first half of the lesson. I enjoy this as it gives you time to be quiet and relax from the strenuous day at school.'

'I'm really pleased with the comment you put on my book last time you marked it. Sarah.'

It's been a wonderful way for me to communicate privately with thirty pupils on a regular basis. I couldn't possibly cope with more than one class at a time using logs, because it is so time-consuming for me to respond effectively. I regret this, for I'm sure it makes me a much better teacher of those thirty individuals, and I would like all my classes to benefit in the same way.

I now explain clearly why we are doing particular things in a particular way. The children's response through the logs allows for much more pupil involvement in what actually happens in the classroom.

Marie Stacey, Court Moor School, Fleet, Hampshire

The final example serves as a reminder that responses may not always be accepted. . .

Tuesday 11th March 1986.

Today I went back to my old work that I was doing. Which was making a sort of mobd bat it went wrong and I then done some sketches to put it right these setthes were.

make it into a half of a churchey bar
or
make it into a land edge with a cliff

I thought about it and I knew it would be hard work for the churcey bar thing so I choose that

That's a great idea Steven! Can you find an advertisement of a crunchy bar to help you with the cobur tests?

NO

Jackie Williams, Oakfield Middle School, Frome, Somerset

For discussion

Start a journal. Share it with your class.

Suggest that your class start a journal. Negotiate with them what sort of journal it might be — who can read it, what could go into it. If you decide that it may be private, make sure that the head and the parents know, understand and agree.

Start a writing log with your class. This is an example from Birchwood School in Cheshire:

What I was asked to do

Give some brief details here about what your teacher wanted you to do eg. We were given a list of ten titles, asked to choose one and then write a story that would fit the title. I chose 'Catastrophe'.

Reflections on my writing

Here you can write about anything that is to do with your writing. Depending on what happened, you might like to comment on: whether you were keen to begin

how you got your ideas

how you set about putting these ideas on paper

what went well with your writing

what difficulties you encountered and how you dealt with these

what help you got

whether, if you had a plan, how far you kept to this plan

whether you wrote the piece straight out or whether you worked in draft form

if you did the latter, what sort of changes you made

how enjoyable or unpleasant you found the writing task

how satisfied you were with what you had written.

These are only suggestions — you may write as little or as much as you wish and about anything that seems of interest and/or importance to you as you reflect on what and how you wrote.

If you wish to write more, continue on the back of this sheet →

The teacher's comments and my response to them

Briefly note the teacher's response to your writing here — perhaps give the mark and comments you received. What were your thoughts about what was said?

What I was asked to do

Reflections on my writing

$\longrightarrow$

The teacher's comments and my response to them

Discuss whether colleagues might co-operate in keeping a simple writing log to try to build up a map of the writing that your pupils do every week.

Teachers' comments

'I have always encouraged children to comment directly to me at the end of any written work. I felt this would be a valuable extension of that idea. Sometimes it helps form a bond between pupil and teacher which can later develop into a spoken conversation; this doesn't always happen with a reticent pupil in a short lesson.'

Reflections on individual pieces of writing

We do not generally learn merely by doing. We learn by doing and then reflecting on what we have done. It is all too easy for us as teachers to monopolise the role of reviewing the success of a pupil's activity, thus weakening a vital link in the learning process.

After pupils have finished a piece of work they might like to reflect on how it happened. This questionnaire might be used as a basis.

'How did you start?

Where did your ideas come from?

What ideas did you reject? Why?

What pleased you most about this piece of work?

What difficulties did you meet?

What was the hardest part to write?

What was the easiest?

What changes did you make at the revision stage? Why?

What is your final feeling about the work?'

Opportunities can be made available to pupils to clarify their intentions, to express their concerns or pleasures about a piece of writing, or to indicate their need for support.

Such opportunities can be built into writing tasks, as in the case of the class of eleven-year-olds in Shropshire who were involved in the production of thematic poetry anthologies which were to include poems both by published poets and by the pupils themselves. Additionally, the pupils were asked to provide a commentary or explanation for each poem they chose to include.

One girl chose to produce an anthology on the theme of 'Animals'. One of her own poems is reproduced here.

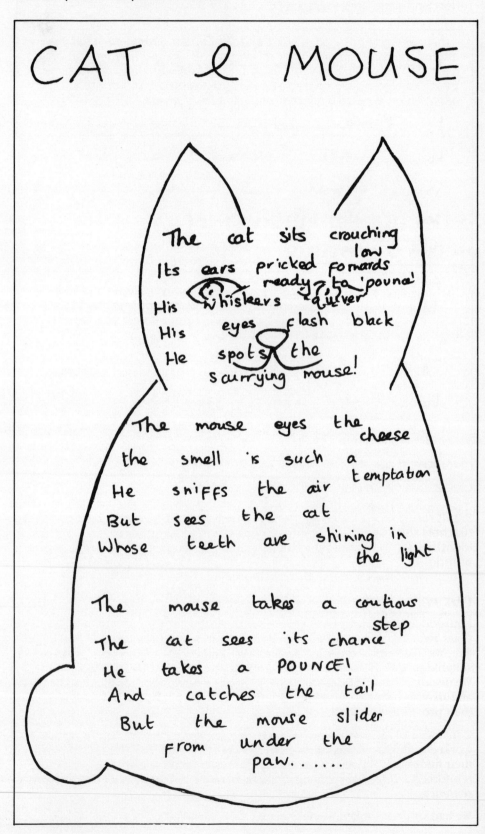

CAT & MOUSE

The cat sits crouching low
Its ears pricked forwards
ready to 'pounce'
His whiskers quiver
His eyes flash black
He spots the scurrying mouse!

The mouse eyes the cheese
the smell is such a temptation
He sniffs the air
But sees the cat
Whose teeth are shining in the light

The mouse takes a cautious step
The cat sees its chance
He takes a POUNCE!
And catches the tail
But the mouse slider
from under the paw......

The writing which accompanied the poem provides an interesting example from a writer given the opportunity to provide the history of the writing and reflect on it, and beginning a dialogue with the teacher.

Commentary on 'Cat and Mouse'

I think one of the reasons why I chose to write about a cat and a mouse is because I have got a cat and see its expressions, the round black eyes, the ears pricked forward etc. I am fond of mice and didn't want to end the poem with it being killed. This was a difficult task because I couldn't say 'And the mouse got away' instead I had to give the empression that it 'only just' got away. I treid many variations and am still not satisfied with my last line.

Pupils rarely receive such an opportunity. Faced with a child's poem, too many teachers tend to determine the strengths and weaknesses of the piece and identify useful changes which might be made. In effect, they take over the writing.

On reflection

I introduced my fourth years to the idea of writing for the very young children of Class Two. As a group, we discussed the type of writing younger children might like. We discussed the textual content, the range of vocabulary and the most suitable type of illustration. We spoke with one voice — *'Keep it simple!'*
We decided it would be useful to look at the picture books actually read by five- and six-year-olds. The budding authors of the fourth year had not yet talked with their prospective readers.

Convinced of the attributes of a 'good' picture story book, my fourth years worked together, criticising material already published. In pairs, they reported their findings to the rest of the class. With each comment, the ideas were reinforced — *'Keep the content simple and leave out the long words and complex sentences.'*

We had still not spoken to the five- and six-year-olds!

Fired with enthusiasm, my class of writers embarked upon the task of making a

Sue Cannell's fourth year Juniors wrote stories for Infants. This exposed them to literary criticism both from their partner and from a critical audience. They were, though, given the opportunity to reflect on how to deal with this criticism. The subsequent interview with the Shropshire Co-ordinator, Ned Ratcliffe, shows how they had developed their understanding.

picture book. *'Keep the vocabulary simple. Keep the sentence structure simple. Don't overcomplicate the plot.'* Little did we know!

The desire to simplify was such that the work the children initially produced was disappointing. It lacked sparkle, interest and any worthwhile content. The oversimplification seemed to have destroyed any flow. I was horrified. Something had to be done to bring the stories alive. We needed to rethink and redraft.

I decided that the children needed a framework within which to work. I devised planning sheets which gave the children the opportunity to think of their stories in terms of pictures. I thought this would make the redrafting process less of a chore.

After reading the new drafts I still felt dissatisfied with the quality of the writing. It did not compare with previous work.

If we had actually spoken with the younger children, the stories might have been better. We might have realised that we had been wrong in assuming that the younger children needed very simple stories. However, as a result of this false start, the fourth years became involved in a variety of situations devised to help them improve their writing. They worked in groups and with partners. They were asked to read their work aloud.

Rebecca did not take kindly to suggestions from her partner about how her story might be improved and she ignored them:

'I didn't like it at first. I took no notice at first.'

She volunteered, though, when there was an opportunity to give a trial reading of her story to a group of Infants. Their response was not as she had anticipated.

'They didn't like it. They said, "Mmmm . . . a bit short . . . Not enough interesting words . . . Make it longer." And they wanted a bit of make-believe in it.'

'It was very embarrassing. I felt . . . hmm . . . if they don't like that, I'm not doing any more. Then I thought, everybody's writing much better stories. I'm going to try . . . so I made an effort.'

After this experience with the Infants, she took more notice of her partner but she still didn't change anything if she felt the original was all right. This was apparent when she and her partner Ruth were interviewed.

Rebecca: *'Some things my partner said, I disagreed with.'*

Ned: *'What do you do, then, if there's something your partner says and you disagree?'*

Ruth: *'Well, you sometimes look at it from different angles, but it doesn't always work. You still keep arguing. But if it's your story you put it how you think best, but don't completely forget the comments.'*

Rebecca's writing told the story of Jane, a little girl who desperately wanted to buy a doll's house she had seen in a toy shop window. She returned home to see if she had sufficient money in her piggy bank. She hadn't.

'Jane lifted up her piggy bank. One single penny fell to the table and Jane's tears fell with it.'

The last sentence was the one that Rebecca said she liked best. She used the falling tears to introduce her imaginary land.

> As Jane's tears fell, a very weird and wonderful thing happened. A sparkling pool of tears had collected on the table and where they had formed, a dark hole appeared. There was a rushing and Jane flew into the darkness below.

Apart from the introduction of fantasy there were other changes to her original story.

'I've changed just about all of it. I thought they wouldn't understand big words — just wanted babyish words — but they didn't want it babyish.'

Rebecca felt that she had changed her views in a number of ways in the course of writing her story for the Infants. She now saw drafting as something potentially useful — *'Don't think you'll get it right first time'* — whereas previously she had seen it as an unnecessary chore. She saw the value of sharing her writing during the process but was also determined that neither of these influences should get in the way of her ownership of the writing.

The experience of producing a story for Infants had been helpful in enabling Rebecca to become more aware of herself as a writer. I'd like to think, too, that Rebecca gained from the opportunity to reflect on the experience and on her writing — an opportunity we rarely seem to give our pupils. Rebecca was a writer who:

- had learned from her audience

- had learned from her peers

- no longer saw drafting merely as a 'rough copy' at the insistence of the teacher

- had been provided with supportive structures

She was also developing a more self-critical outlook, learning from the experience by having the opportunity to talk about it and reflect on it.

Rebecca wrote to her reader:

Dear Freya,
                All books are different
as you will find out when you read
them. You open the book and read,
a new world is before you. Book World
you might call it.
          I wrote this book for you and
you were in my mind day and
night. Enjoy this book and keep it
for your children and let their children
read it,

                    Lots of Love

                              Rebecca Pote.

Sue Cannell, Church Stretton C. of E. Primary School, Shropshire
and Ned Ratcliffe, Shropshire Writing Project Co-ordinator

Further examples of ways of helping children to reflect on their work can be found in other Theme Packs. See, in particular, *Writing and Learning* Section 2: Reflecting and responding.

For discussion

This questionnaire, or variations on it, might be offered to your class as a basis for discussion.

As a writer, how can you tell if your writing is good?

As a reader, what do you like or look for in a piece of writing?

What might make your writing better?

What difference does it make to your judgement if you know the writer?

One way in which these questions could be used is as follows:

1   Distribute the questions and ask everyone to brainstorm their ideas on to the sheets.

2   After about ten minutes, divide the class into small groups of three or four to discuss their immediate reactions to the questions. Ask each group to make a rough list which incorporates the ideas of the group.

3   A class list could then be compiled from the various group lists, leading to the production of a poster or a sheet to be kept in the writing folder/writing book.

The following issues should be raised during the discussions:

- different meanings of the term 'writing' (handwriting/content/ surface appearance)

- the idea of 'good' in relation to the individual's history/the class/ some absolute standard

- the criteria that can be used to judge a text

- function (does it do the job?) — format (is it clear?) — audience (is it appropriate?)

Janet White, NFER

This questionnaire was developed by the Avon Writing Project.

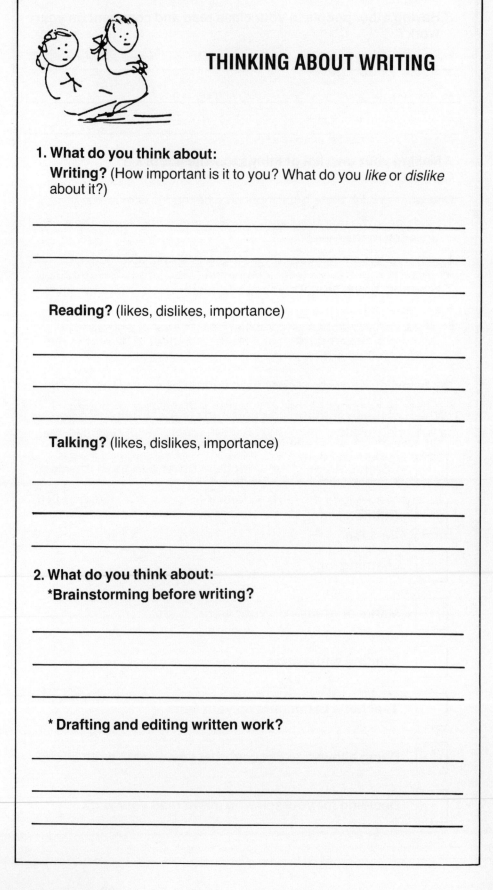

THINKING ABOUT WRITING

1. What do you think about:

Writing? (How important is it to you? What do you *like* or *dislike* about it?)

_____

_____

_____

Reading? (likes, dislikes, importance)

_____

_____

_____

Talking? (likes, dislikes, importance)

_____

_____

_____

2. What do you think about:
   *Brainstorming before writing?

_____

_____

_____

* Drafting and editing written work?

_____

_____

_____

* **Having other people in your class read and comment on your work?**

_____

_____

_____

* **Making your own list of things to write about?**

_____

_____

_____

* **Keeping a 'learning log'?**

_____

_____

_____

3. **Which of these activities do you think is most helpful to you as a writer?** (Please number the boxes in order of importance to you.)

☐   **Comments on your work from other people in the class**

☐   **Brainstorming**

☐   **Learning logs**

☐   **Marks or grades on your work**

☐   **Drafting and editing**

☐   **Teacher's comments on your work**

☐   **Being allowed to choose what you want to write about**

☐   **Deciding for yourself who might read your work**

4. Do you find writing difficult?

_____

_____

_____

**5. Is the way you write, read or talk in English different from the
way you do these things in other subjects?**

_____

_____

_____

**6. Has your way of writing changed over the past two years at
school?**

— ⟶ — | 198/ | ⟶ — ⟶ — | 198/ | ⟶ — ⟶

_____

_____

_____

**7. Which piece of your English work this year are you most
pleased with or proud of?** (Please describe this piece and explain
why you've chosen it.)

_____

_____

_____

_____

_____

_____

_____

_____

_____

8. Please use this space if there are any other comments you would
like to make about the writing you have done this year (for example,
keeping your own writing folder; using sketches and photographs to
illustrate your writing; using 'top sheets' for evaluating your writing;
choosing readers for your writing).

Hengrove Comprehensive School
National Writing Project in Avon
June 1987

We need to ensure that we provide writers with the means and the opportunity to exercise more control over both the process and the products of writing. Writers need to be able to make choices and decisions for themselves in a range of ways. They can establish their own criteria for judging the effectiveness of a particular piece of writing. Both the process of arriving at such criteria and the criteria themselves will be helpful to individual writers.

Mark it yourself

I discussed with my class of twelve- to thirteen-year-olds the results of the school survey of children's views on writing. We decided to formulate some questions which would help them to evaluate their own and other children's writing. We discussed this in relation to their use of redrafting, and they put forward a number of questions which they thought would be helpful in the writing of factual pieces. I simply recorded these as they were mentioned; then, as a class, we put them into the order in which we felt they should be asked. One child then wrote them out on a large piece of paper and pinned them up for everyone to refer to when necessary. The questions were:

1 Does it make sense?

2 Is it set out well; are the diagrams clear?

3 Is the information in the right order?

4 Is it accurate?

5 If children's own ideas have been included, are they relevant?

6 Have punctuation and spelling been considered?

Punctuation and spelling were placed last because the children felt that their importance should not be overstressed. This was a response to the survey in which children had ranked punctuation and spelling relatively highly.

We applied these questions and the collaborative approach to our writing about sex education and relationships. We found, though, that the questions were not as appropriate when looking at imaginative writing or poetry. We had another class discussion and the children produced a slightly different set of questions which they thought were more appropriate to this type of writing. These were:

1 Can the choice of words be improved?

2 Does it make sense?

3 Is it set out well?

4 Is it too long or too short?

5 Are the ideas in the right order?

6 Is there a catchy beginning and a decent ending?

7 Have punctuation and spelling been considered?

On the whole, this approach to the evaluation by the children of their own and each others' work was accepted with enthusiasm.

Sue Apted, Stirchley Middle School, Shropshire

What response do you want?	When might you want it?
1. Talk about your ideas. What have you done so far; how will you proceed?	At an early stage or when something fresh is happening.
2. Read aloud with no feedback at all.	Any time when you would like to know what the writing sounds like in the presence of others but aren't ready for their reactions.
3. *Active listening* The listener tries to say, in his/her own words, what the writer is getting at, and allows the writer to say more. 'So, are you saying that..?'	You want to find out if you are making the points you think you are.
4. *Pointing feedback* What words or images stand out for you as a reader? Don't say how or why it affected you; just point to whatever you can in the text.	You want some confirmation to know you have made an impression – but you are not ready for more specific feedback.
5. *Suggestions* 'If I were writing this I would… because I…'	Late in the process, and only if you find it easy to say 'no'.
6. How does this piece of writing work/not work for you?	Late, if you want to perfect it.
7. *Proofreading and editing* Look for places where the mechanics make you feel uncomfortable, and point these out to the writer, even if you don't know what's wrong.	Only when ready for the final draft.

These strategies for self-evaluation are all, to an extent, dependent on an understanding of the writing process and the options that are available within it. One form of self-evaluation is to become aware of the kinds of response you require. Here is a menu of possibilities adapted from Robert Whitney's sheets for the New York Writing Project.

There is no single model of the writing process, either for all writers or for all tasks. However, if writers have a vocabulary with which to understand what they are doing, if they can think about the complex system of writing in terms of manageable stages, then they are more likely to be in control.

Starting writing	Establishing the purpose, getting ideas, deciding on format and audience
Composing	Getting the ideas into a text
Revising	Finding out whether the text does its job and amending it if necessary
Editing	Polishing the text to make it easy to read
Publishing	Letting the piece reach its audience
Evaluation	Reflecting on the piece of writing in order to learn from it and perhaps tackle the next piece better

Here is one model which has been used and refined by the Avon Writing Project.

For discussion

Different aspects of the writing process will require different responses. What sort of response is required in each case? (You could use this plan.)

Activity	What aspect is being responded to? (Ideas? Content? Surface features?)	Who could do it? (Writer? Peers? Teacher? Someone else?)	How is it being done? (Spoken at the time? Spoken afterwards? Written?)	What is its purpose? (More ideas? Correction? Trouble-shooting?)
Starting writing				
Composing				
Revising				
Editing				
Publishing				
Evaluation				

Does your practice match your views? What organisational difficulties are there? Which of them can be overcome?

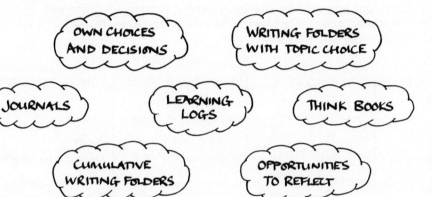

IF DEVELOPING WRITERS ARE OFFERED...

OWN CHOICES AND DECISIONS

WRITING FOLDERS WITH TOPIC CHOICE

JOURNALS

LEARNING LOGS

THINK BOOKS

CUMULATIVE WRITING FOLDERS

OPPORTUNITIES TO REFLECT

... WHAT IS LIKELY TO EMERGE?

- an explicit understanding of the writing process
- control of and responsibility for the writing process
- generation and self-direction of their own writing
- a broad understanding of what writing can do
- a sense of their own development as writers
- comparison of past and present performance
- reflection on their own development
- assessment of both process and products
- a growing awareness of their achievements
- acquisition of a vocabulary with which to discuss their writing with others
- development of criteria by which to evaluate their writing
- questions about their writing which they and others can address

Teachers in the Mid Glamorgan Writing Project summarised their work on 'Writing reflections' in this diagram.

5 Changing other people's ideas

When teachers start to question how they respond to their pupils' writing, there will be implications which affect not only the pupils, but also parents, other classes and other teachers.

Teachers' comments

'The reaction from most other teachers was that what I had embarked on didn't concern them. One teacher did show interest in the questionnaire I had drawn up, so I'm hoping for some feedback when he gives the same questionnaire to his class.'

Sue Dashouri from Birmingham writes about how her school tackled the way in which writing was being approached and assessed.

A positive approach

When our school became involved in the Writing Project, the first thing the Infant representative and I decided was that we didn't really know much about the writing that went on in the school, so we needed to do some information gathering. There was a general staff meeting to explain the Project and, for organisational and timetable reasons, future meetings were arranged separately for the Infant and the Junior staff.

We decided that we would begin by finding out more about:

- what sort and what standard of writing was going on throughout the school
- how teachers approached writing, especially free writing
- the ways in which writing was marked and assessed

All teachers were asked to supply pieces of work from three or four children to show the range of writing levels within each class. These samples were duplicated and distributed to staff at the meetings.

Then the work from each class was discussed in detail. At first, the discussions tended to take the form of criticism, concentrating on the mistakes and negative aspects of each piece of work such as poor spelling, lack of punctuation and wrong use of tenses. A different approach was suggested, consisting of these central ideas:

- read the work as it is, listening for the voice of the child sounding through
- look for the positive points — what has this child attempted and achieved?
- look for the growing points — the points at which support or instruction would be most appropriate and effective

Concern and uncertainty were expressed about marking spelling, grammar and punctuation, and it was decided that a school policy needed to be developed to cover all these issues. Rather than staff being told that a new policy was needed, or being handed a policy statement, an awareness of the need developed out of staff discussion.

Both representatives took on the role of organiser with at least a little apprehension, but the staff response, both in staff meetings and informally, has given both of us a great deal of encouragement. The approach to children's writing has taken a more positive direction, and in discussion staff now tend to look for the good points first. A great deal of time has been spent examining individual pieces of work, a luxury that is not often afforded to a busy class teacher. Sometimes only two pieces of work have been discussed in one session of twenty to thirty minutes. Staff have been willing to discuss work in depth, questioning what the child was really trying to express.

The question of marking is still being discussed. It has been generally agreed among staff that free writing, either personal or imaginative, should not be covered with red ink and that a positive comment written by the teacher would be more useful. The staff were also in agreement that the ideal way to mark a piece of work is to do so with the child present, and any written comments should reflect the oral response given by the teacher. This is not always practicable in a busy classroom, but a teacher's written comment might be in the form of a question for the child to answer, perhaps about the story content. This could set up a written dialogue and emphasise the teacher's role as a reader rather than merely an assessor. Mistakes would be noted by the teacher but not on the child's writing. The idea of correcting a minor error in pencil was thought to be feasible, and common mistakes for a group or class could thus be the basis for future lessons.

A common problem experienced by teachers is the time children spend waiting for spellings to be written by the teacher in their dictionaries. This was thought to hinder children's writing flow and many of the staff are currently trying a new approach. Children are told that they will not be given spellings but that they should try for themselves.

There is no doubt that a change is taking place in our attitude to writing. Many of the staff have found that the 'no-spellings-given' idea has led to more relaxed writing sessions. After the initial shock, the children have adapted to this and no longer ask for words but concentrate on the writing. In most cases, staff have been surprised by the high standard of independent spelling. Children do have specific lessons where spelling is taught, and it seems that some of what they learn then is transferred to their writing if they are encouraged to try spellings for themselves. Teachers are trying several other new approaches to writing:

- letting the children write on their own initiative rather than having a lengthy introduction and build-up by the teacher

- encouraging groups of children to talk and write together

- encouraging children to read their work privately to other children or aloud to the teacher and the class

We feel we need more observation and experiment before a marking policy is agreed and written down, but staff have commented that their children enjoy reading the teachers' comments and that this approach to marking has made them more positive in their attitude to a child's attempts. There is now considerable interest in the school in how children's writing develops. Teachers have often sent pieces of work to other staff to read and many informal discussions have taken place during the school day.

To summarise: there has been a marked increase in enthusiasm for and discussion about writing throughout the school. Teachers have shared ideas, successes and failures and have also had the confidence to experiment and try out new ways of approaching writing. There is a long way to go, but we have been encouraged by the positive approach now taken towards writing.

I hope that this spirit is being conveyed to the children, and will be reflected in their writing development and in their enthusiasm for writing.

Sue Dashouri, St. James C. of E. School, Handsworth, Birmingham

Jackie Kidd describes a session at her school where response to writing was discussed.

Responses to writing — a framework for personal reflection and staff discussion

I claim no more for this framework than that it was of great value to me personally as a way of clarifying purposeful ways of developing responses to the writing of children in my class. However, it did provide a basis for some useful staff discussion, and in this capacity I hope it may be of use to readers of this article.

Ideally, two staff sessions would be planned, since issues discussed at the first meeting may well need to be considered by staff before strategies to be added to school policy are agreed. Ideas may then be further developed through discussion.

1 Before staff discussion

- Give out photocopies of 'A way of looking at children's writing' by Ned Ratcliffe and John Richmond.

- Staff involved in the discussion use this to assess some writing in their class.

- Children's writing and teachers' documentation of how the writing was organised should be brought to the discussion.

2 The discussion: responding to children's writing

This is worked through in four parts:

Labels

- What labels do we honestly attach to the act of responding to children's writing? For example: *'looking at', 'marking', 'correcting', 'assessing'*

- Is it useful to decide on one term which accurately describes our practices — the meaning of which should be understood by all (parents, teachers, children)?

- Should that word be *'responding'*?

Practices

- What do we actually do when responding to children's writing?
  For example: correct spelling, add full stops, always add a positive comment, help child to focus thoughts?
  Having discussed what we actually do and having established individual justifications for those practices, we may make suggestions to help children enjoy writing and develop their ability to do so qualitatively.

- Do we respond positively to writing as often as we could/should?

- Do we encourage/allow children to respond to their own/a friend's writing as often as we should?

- Could staff pair up to respond to their classwork on a half-termly basis?

Suggestions evolved through the group discussion are considered and a list of strategies agreed, to be practised by all members of staff until the second meeting. The merits and demerits of practices can then be discussed more fully in the light of people's experiences before a set of strategies is agreed by all.

Problems

- If responding sensitively to writing is seen as very time-consuming, we must decide upon our priorities and agree what is feasible.

- Can responding to a child's work in the child's absence be of any value to the child's developing ability to write? Does this depend on the age of the child?

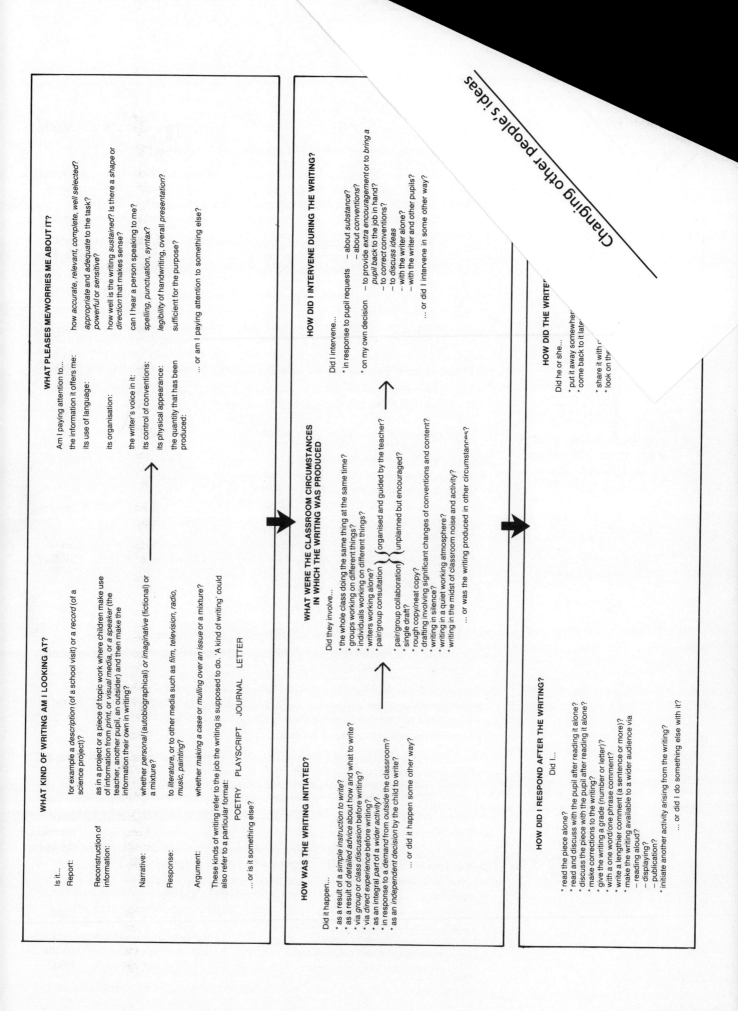

WHAT KIND OF WRITING AM I LOOKING AT?

Is it...

Report: for example a description (of a school visit) or a record (of a science project)?

Reconstruction of information: as in a project or a piece of topic work where children make use of information from print, or visual media, or a speaker (the teacher, another pupil, an outsider) and then make the information their own in writing?

Narrative: whether personal (autobiographical) or imaginative (fictional) or a mixture?

Response: to literature, or to other media such as film, television, radio, music, painting?

Argument: whether making a case or mulling over an issue or a mixture?

These kinds of writing refer to the job the writing is supposed to do. 'A kind of writing' could also refer to a particular format:

POETRY   PLAYSCRIPT   JOURNAL   LETTER

... or is it something else?

WHAT PLEASES ME/WORRIES ME ABOUT IT?

Am I paying attention to...

the information it offers me: how accurate, relevant, complete, well selected? appropriate and adequate to the task? powerful or sensitive?

its use of language: how well is the writing sustained? Is there a shape or direction that makes sense?

its organisation: can I hear a person speaking to me?

the writer's voice in it: spelling, punctuation, syntax?

its control of conventions: legibility of handwriting, overall presentation?

its physical appearance: sufficient for the purpose?

the quantity that has been produced:

... or am I paying attention to something else?

HOW DID I INTERVENE DURING THE WRITING?

Did I intervene...

* in response to pupil requests – about substance?
                                  – about conventions?
* on my own decision – to provide extra encouragement or to bring a pupil back to the job in hand?
                      – to correct conventions?
                      – to discuss ideas
                      – with the writer alone?
                      – with the writer and other pupils?

... or did I intervene in some other way?

WHAT WERE THE CLASSROOM CIRCUMSTANCES IN WHICH THE WRITING WAS PRODUCED

Did they involve...

* the whole class doing the same thing at the same time?
* groups working on different things?
* individuals working on different things?
* writers working alone?
* pair/group consultation
* pair/group collaboration   } organised and guided by the teacher? unplanned but encouraged?
* single draft?
* rough copy/neat copy?
* writing in silence?
* writing in a quiet working atmosphere?
* writing in the midst of classroom noise and activity?

... or was the writing produced in other circumstances?

HOW WAS THE WRITING INITIATED?

Did it happen...

* as a result of a simple instruction to write?
* as a result of detailed advice about how and what to write?
* via group or class discussion before writing?
* via direct experience before writing?
* as an integral part of a wider activity?
* in response to a demand from outside the classroom?
* as an independent decision by the child to write?

... or did it happen some other way?

HOW DID I RESPOND AFTER THE WRITING?

Did I...

* read the piece alone?
* read and discuss with the pupil after reading it alone?
* discuss the piece with the pupil after reading it alone?
* make corrections to the writing?
* give the writing a grade (number or letter)?
* with a one word/one phrase comment?
* write a lengthier comment (a sentence or more)?
* make the writing available to a wider audience via
  – reading aloud?
  – displaying?
  – publication?
* initiate another activity arising from the writing?

... or did I do something else with it?

HOW DID THE WRITER

Did he or she...

* put it away somewher...
* come back to it late...

* share it with o...
* look on th...

81

Why mark?

- to please the head or the parents, or because we feel that work set in class should be followed up in some way?

- to develop the children's writing?

- to help children to enjoy writing and to want to write?

If we define our reasons for response, we hope we will define how it helps children learn through agreed school response policies.

Jackie Kidd, South View Junior School, Basingstoke, Hampshire

The question most frequently asked by teachers thinking about the effectiveness of their marking policy and contemplating changing it is: what are the parents going to think? Parents are rightly concerned with the development of their children, and if they can be brought into the process of moving thinking forward, they can be considerable allies. There are many ideas about how this can be done in the Theme Pack *Writing Partnerships (1): home, school and community*.

The next account describes a Parents' Evening where marking policy was discussed.

A *writing evening*

At an early stage of the Cheshire Writing Project we examined issues of response to children's writing. We felt the need to be more explicit with parents about our policy and about how they might assist their children. It was too easy, we felt, to criticise parents for an obsession with surface features of writing; what had we done to encourage them to look deeper? At the same time the local Primary schools had become actively involved with us in looking at response.

Our English department was already in the process of trying to set out, for pupils, what its courses involved and why. As part of this process, every fourth year pupil had received in September a GCSE booklet including:

- a description of the course and its requirements

- a form to record the pupil's work and achievement

- a framework for reflection and criticism of the course

The English department decided to hold an evening meeting, about response to writing, which would involve parents, pupils and Primary teachers. We sent letters of invitation explaining the purpose of the evening. Originally, we intended this to be a workshop, but the large response made this impractical. We settled for a mixture of formal talk and group sessions.

On arrival, each person was given a copy of our marking policy and a pamphlet outlining the ways in which we felt parents could help children develop their writing. On display were stories written by seniors for juniors, stories written by younger and older pupils on the same topics, and pupils' comments on writing: where, when and how they like to write, what sorts of response they find valuable, and so on.

In the formal session we presented a brief survey of the writing children do in Junior and Secondary school, indicating the nature, variety and development of writing, and how we try to help pupils to improve, including our provision for special needs. This session explicitly addressed the question of what factors facilitate writing, stressing sense of purpose, sense of audience and drafting. The meeting then broke up into groups to examine a variety of aspects of and approaches to children's writing. In response to parents' questions, some groups moved away from the planned topic.

Group 1 looked at some Primary pupils' writing from initial stimulus through rough drafts to final form. There was discussion of the process, problems and factors which help. Parents were invited to write too — but courteously declined!

Responding to parental questions, Groups 2 and 3 discussed the document 'Our marking policy'. Issues concerning which errors were corrected, and why, were extensively considered.

OUR MARKING POLICY

Marking is of value only if comments are read and regarded. Ideally, marking becomes part of a developing dialogue resulting in pupil progress: a pupil writes, the writing is marked and in his/her subsequent writing, the pupil incorporates suggested improvements or, better still, goes beyond them.

When this pattern is achieved, marking justifies the considerable expertise and time it demands.

Appreciating

Often we express our enthusiasm about or enjoyment of a piece of work: *'This was fun!' 'I really enjoyed the part about…'* We do this to show the pupil that his/her writing has a genuine audience, someone who is interested in what he/she has to say and is not reading the story or essay merely to find fault with it. We can hope that a pupil's writing will improve only if that pupil has a sense that the writing is valued.

Replying

This is an extension of the process of appreciating. We reply to pupils' work by sharing our own experience (*'I know just what you mean here – I've felt upset like this'*), by questioning, by challenging – *'But why did the boy steal? Why did the shopkeeper not call the police? Why do you believe this?'* The reply shows that the writing has a reader and that the reader is not passive but wants to *share* the experiences and the ideas. Part of the sharing is in the form of this written dialogue. By making a pupil aware of the *needs* and response of the reader, we show him/her areas which can be developed and improved.

Improving

Marking is often equated with correcting – indicating errors in spelling, grammar and punctuation – generally in vivid, red ink!

It is our belief that correcting has its place in marking, but *only* in so far as it contributes to the improvement of a pupil's work. Errors need to be pointed out if a pupil is to improve his/her work; which errors and how many will depend, however, on many factors.

Assessing

We constantly assess our pupils' work, establishing their relative abilities and their achievement against national norms.

Groups 4 and 5 considered in detail our document 'Writing: helping at home'.

Writing: helping at home

All writers can benefit from talking about their writing – and this is where parents can really help.

Basically, writers need to know how a piece of writing affects a reader or listener. In what are sometimes called 'writing conferences', writers read what they've written to someone and ask questions to find out if it says what they think it is saying. Listeners ask questions about what they have and haven't heard, helping writers discover what alterations they need to make.

There are some points to bear in mind when responding to your child's writing.

1. **Ask writers to talk through their ideas.**
   Before they write, it is helpful for writers to 'rehearse' what they think they want to put into their piece of writing. Asking *'What are some of the things you're thinking of writing about?'* can help writers get started.

2. **Ask writers to read their writing aloud.**
   Reading aloud helps writers discover things themselves about their writing and makes them aware of their own 'writer's voice'.

3. **Keep in mind the stage of development that the piece of writing has reached.**
   Successive drafts represent developments in thought and perception and the kind of help that's most appropriate will depend on the stage the writing has reached. In the early stages of a piece of writing, writers need to know whether they have all the necessary information; later, they need to know if the reader is clear about what they're saying; finally, they may seek guidance as they proof-read their writing. With young writers who are learning the 'mechanics' of writing (spelling, punctuation, grammar), it is important that *they* do as much of the correcting as possible.

4. **Don't comment on too much!**
   One or two observations may be enough at one time. Frequent short 'conferences' of this nature are better than one long one.

5. **Let writers take the lead.**
   As far as possible, ask writers to say what they want help with. Ask them what *they* think about their piece of writing so that they begin to make the kinds of judgement that mature writers make.

6. **Be honest, positive and specific.**
   Be honest in giving your opinions and make sure that you tell writers which parts of their writing you like and why. Show writers – by asking the questions you have as a reader – precisely where more information or greater clarity is required.

7. **Encourage writers to write and share their writing with you.**
   As a parent, try to encourage your children to share their writing with you and ask your opinions. Writers must see that 'writing conferences' are valuable for them – the more they feel that they gain from talking with you about their writing, the more they will want to do it.

> ### 8. Write yourself.
> The best way to discover how to respond usefully to another writer's work is to become a writer yourself. Why not do some writing, share it with your children and ask them to help you with it?
>
> Growth in writing is strongest when writers are in control, when they 'own' their writing. These points about 'conferencing' can all help writers learn to take responsibility for their work and to make decisions about their writing that will help them grow in self-confidence and skill.

Group 6 focused on fourth year Secondary pupils' discursive writing. First drafts and initial plans for an essay on the place of women in society were circulated. In pairs, members of the group were asked to consider the advice they would offer.

Group 7 examined some descriptive writing by eleven-year-olds; members considered how each writer might be encouraged to develop.

Group 8 observed while two brave fourteen-year-old volunteers had a previously unread piece of their work discussed and marked by their teacher. This led to discussion about what the process of consultation was intended to achieve and about the methods adopted.

Group 9 looked at first drafts of pieces recently written by pupils. In pairs, they were asked to put written comments on each piece, using guidelines designed to help pupils respond positively to each others' work. In this group, as elsewhere, it was stressed that parents were being invited to appreciate, to reply, to suggest improvements — but not to assess work.

The evening concluded informally with parents looking at materials used in other groups and discussing individual worries and problems.

Reflections

There were aspects of the evening which could have been improved. For example, the large numbers limited discussion although we were delighted and surprised that 250 parents attended. Most importantly, the evening was presented as an 'English' evening, perhaps giving the misleading impression that writing is a matter for the English department only. However, it was a friendly and rewarding experience, even if we felt that issues had only been raised and not examined in depth. There was a strong sense that everyone present wanted to work together for the good of the pupils. Parents were encouraged to follow up the evening with their own children, and an open invitation was extended to visit the schools and see our work.

A vital development, as yet insufficiently planned, is to extend discussion of the issues raised at the writing evening to all departments within the school.

Paul Twambley, Leftwich High School, Northwich, Cheshire

Ned Ratcliffe has used the following story as a starting point with groups of teachers in order to encourage them to think of ways of responding to what a child can do. The story was produced by Kate, a five-year-old in Dee Snape's class in Church Stretton Primary School, Shropshire. She was one of a small group of children who had been brought together for an hour a week to produce a story for the fourth year Juniors.

Showing what they can do

Kate's story

'One day my mummy was not well so I help her. Then at nite time i went to bed. and I herd her talking. In the morning she was better And she said I cood go to the petshop. i bote the prettiest bird ans asekd of I cood bring it up to my bedroom and she I cood so I did. i was looking at its pritty tail and I fownd a nise fether. I pulld it. It chanjd. its legs groow first. They were slimy yellow spotty spiky legs. Then its body groow. It was slimy. Then its hede groow. and there were antennis. They sprawled up and glowd when he was fritnd. I took 9 steps back He took 9 steps fowd Then I took 1 step back he took 1 step fowd. Then just as i was going to run it said I like you.

Then suddenly it wantid me to go on his back. It said to me wood you like to come with me to jopiter I said to him okay but how do i get there. clime into 1 of my antennis and ther shood be some controwls there. bhut how do I get in your antenni. i shull make a spell. i sudnley felt myself shoot upwoods then i climd in to a antenni i pulld a lever he sundunly becam invizubl and went upwoods in one minit we had landid on jopiter. it lookd straj from Eruth. Just then I hurd music it was music from Eruth I jumpd up and down The music was bring me back to Euth. i sad good buy and my mum was glad to see me home agen. She said wer have you been.'

Kate's story is presented just as it was first written. Nothing has been changed. It has simply been typeset for ease of reading.

A question I have asked various groups of teachers in considering the story is this:

What, in these circumstances, has Kate demonstrated to us that she is able to do as a writer?

You may like to re-read her story and jot down your responses to the question before moving on to read a summary of aspects of other teachers' responses.

You may find it helpful to answer the question in terms of:

Substance — focusing on matters such as the content, the organisation, the language

System — focusing on matters such as spelling, syntax, punctuation and other conventions of writing

As you might expect, there was a tremendous range of responses to the writing. We do not all 'read' it in the same way. However, a sharing of responses often leads to new insights into the writing. Emphasising the positive — what Kate can do rather than what she isn't able to yet, or doesn't demonstrate in this particular piece of writing — is vital. Too often, perhaps, our classroom response to writing emphasises what needs to be put right rather than valuing what is there.

The analysis which follows is not intended to be comprehensive — you may find that you have focused on aspects of the writing which are not mentioned here. What follows is simply a summary of the comments of the various groups of teachers who have had the opportunity to respond to the writing.

There can be little doubt that Kate is a confident writer — unusually so for a five-year-old, some teachers felt. In her story she demonstrates extensive knowledge of how stories work, of how they are organised and structured, of the conventions which frequently operate, and of how these relate to the needs and expectations of readers.

Her story is both simple and sophisticated. It has an extended plot, in a number of locations or settings. It has a recognisable beginning and end. The plot is more than a sequence of events or episodes. The events of her story are linked causally — one thing leads to another. The story is a fantasy which is firmly rooted in reality — it begins and ends in the security and comfort of home.

The story is written in the first person and this is sustained throughout. Kate makes use of both reported and direct speech. She appears to prefer direct speech when she considers the matter to be of greater importance. For example:

'she said I cood go to the petshop'

but

'clime into 1 of my antennis and there shood be some controwls there. bhut how do I get in your antenni'

This conversation moves the action on, but it also begins to express feelings. In one case in particular the use of actual words spoken rather than of reported speech has a considerable effect.

Consider the impact of:

'Then just as i was going to run it said I like you'

as opposed to a version she could have chosen:

'Then just as I was going to run it said that it liked me.'

Kate manages mood and pace remarkably well, too. She makes selective use of description and detail, including a great deal about the bird's appearance and growth, for example. There is also variety in her choice of adjectives and verbs:

'prettiest' . . . 'pritty' . . . 'nise' . . . 'slimy yellow' . . . 'spotty' . . . 'spiky' . . . 'sprawted' . . . 'glowd' . . . 'clime' . . . 'shoot'

She sustains our interest and builds in elements of surprise. Consider, for example, her handling of the sequence of events from the pulling of the *'nise fether'* to *'I like you'*. Here, rhythm, repetition and variety of sentence length and pattern all contribute to a building up of tension only released by the words *'I like you'*.

'I pulld it.
It chanjd.
its legs groow first.
. . .
Then its body groow.
. . .
Then its hede groow.
. . .
I took 9 steps back
He took 9 steps fowd
Then I took 1 step back
he took 1 step fowd
Then just as i was going to run . . .'

Kate also handles time with remarkable ease in her story, both in the vocabulary she uses to indicate passage of time and in the amount of time she devotes to particular incidents. So we have:

'One day . . . Then at nite time . . .
In the morning . . . first . . .
Then . . . Then . . . suddenly
in one minit . . .
Just then . . . wer have you been.'

These devices help to shape the story in time and space for the reader.

Comment has already been made on Kate's choice of sentence structure and its effect. There are other aspects worthy of comment too. Kate makes use of a variety of sentence lengths, usually to good effect. She shows herself capable of fairly complex structures, as in the final sentence of the first paragraph. She also uses questions — one from the bird, one of her own, and one from her mother to provide the ending.

Another interesting feature of her writing relates to word order. Consider, for example, the difference brought about by the placement of the word *'suddenly'* in the following sentences.

'Then suddenly it wanted me to go on his back.'

'. . . sudnley felt myself shoot upwoods'

When we turn our attention to Kate's handling of the *system* of written language, her achievement is again impressive. In what is a fairly lengthy story, using a wide range of vocabulary, more than 80% of the words are spelled correctly and few teachers had any difficulties in reading any words which are not. Kate writes in sentences, many of which are correctly marked with capital letters and full stops. The one division she makes into paragraphs comes at a particularly appropriate moment in the story.

I make no apology for:

- emphasising composition (getting and arranging ideas) above transcription (spelling, punctuation, handwriting)

- focusing positively on what Kate has done, rather than on the extent to which she has failed to produce a conventional adult product

The summary reflects both the balance of what teachers have said, and the relative attention we should pay to composition and transcription when dealing with emerging writers. I want to emphasise the importance of seeing Kate and other, less confident, writers as *developing* writers and not as *failing* writers.

So what can we make of Kate's achievement? Given the extent and range of understanding, knowledge and experience which she demonstrates, what are the implications for us as classroom teachers in terms of the provision we might make for other developing writers?

Probably one of the best starting points is to ask where Kate gets her knowledge, understanding and awareness of:

- story convention and structure

- print conventions

- readership

- word choice

- sentence structures and patterns

What should become clear is how little will have come through instruction, and how much will have come through experience of stories told and stories read. You may even feel that you recognise particular picture book stories in phrases that Kate has used, in the pattern of events or in the ending of her story. It is precisely the kind of experience of talk and text that Kate is able to draw upon in writing her story that we need to make available to all our emerging writers. An integration of talking, reading and writing, purposeful contexts, and a rich literary environment are essential to developing writers.

Ned Ratcliffe, Shropshire Writing Project Co-ordinator

Appendix

Ways of looking at children's writing: The National Writing Project response to the Task Group on Assessment and Testing (TGAT)

The National Writing Project was asked by TGAT for information and suggestions about the assessment of writing, drawing on the experiences of practising teachers and their advisers.

Hundreds of teachers in the Project have been observing children writing and analysing their written texts. In some cases this has involved an intense, systematic study of a few individual children; in others, a less formal monitoring of the achievements of a class in writing. One important conclusion reached by all participants in the Project is that writing is a highly complex social practice which cannot be reduced to any simple list of terms or criteria, and that writers cannot be assessed by one-off tests at particular ages. This is not to dismiss the concept of assessment but to interpret assessment as an integral part of the writing curriculum. Indicated below are some of the emphases which we hope will be reflected in any national assessment of writing.

1   What can the child write?

A major emphasis in our approach is placed on finding out what children are able to write rather than what they cannot write. Such assessment of achievement is well illustrated in examples from the early years. The child who writes:

'I like playing in the water'   *Lee*

. . . at age five demonstrates considerable knowledge about writing: that print conveys a message; that is it used to describe one's reaction; that separate symbols represent words; that there is some (as yet unclear) relationship between letters and sounds; that writing goes from left to right, and so on.

Another child wrote:

'The Hulk is standing on a snake and Batman has got his pole'

. . . demonstrating much knowledge of writing but different hypotheses from those of Lee about the adult system. His strategy of beginning his message with some sort of 'practice' letter strings reflects an experimental approach to writing development characteristic of early writers.

We begin by looking at these two pieces of writing in order to show how much can be and needs to be said about children's writing ability. A teacher (or parent, employer or other adult) needs to be informed about a child's progress in writing, but this information must come from frequent observations of children engaged in writing. Such observations need to recognise the child's experiments with what is known about adult writers' uses of language and to see these as points of development rather than examples of failure.

In the early years especially, only frequent observations can capture the major developments that take place in children's writing. An extreme (but not exceptional) example demonstrates this need for regular sampling. A seven-year-old wrote:

This was a representative piece of her writing. Six weeks later, the child wrote about her trip to the dentist, using lines when she was unsure of the spelling.

(The text continued for ten more lines.)

Such development would be missed if the teacher were using a method of assessment which failed to look at development across a period of time.

2   Which conditions promote the best writing?

Assessment cannot be considered in a vacuum; rather, it forms an integral part of critical reflection about the curriculum. The Project has countless examples to demonstrate that success in writing depends on the context in which learning takes place. Our activities provide evidence to show that confidence and competence develop best when the writing is for a specific audience and purpose; when the child has control over what is written, when and for whom; when the child becomes aware of the behaviours involved in writing such as drafting and editing; and when each child's contribution is fully valued.

We would wish to argue that any assessment procedure should not be separate from a development procedure in which teachers can evaluate the opportunities provided in the writing curriculum. Furthermore, we would argue that alongside any identification of children's ability should be accounts of the environment in which their writing development was supported.

3   Which types of writing need to be considered?

There is no one type of writing which can represent a writer's ability, nor is it possible to reduce writing ability to a set of isolated components. Neither a monolithic nor a reductive model of language learning is acceptable. The evidence from the National Writing Project and from the NFER Assessment of Performance Unit underlines the idea that writing performance is strongly related to the nature of the task. A wide range of writing tasks should therefore be included in any assessment, and it should be recognised that different tasks need different kinds of assessment.

4   What expectations are there for a writer's development?

As children get older their writing generally improves. They gain greater control over the conventions of writing (spelling, punctuation); they have more stamina for extended texts; they have more access to different types of writing; they are more able to adapt their writing according to the purposes and audience; and they have more confidence in the process of writing with the ability to reflect on their writing behaviour.

Having said that about development we do not feel that it is possible or desirable to provide a series of development markers which will differentiate a five-year-old's writing from that of an eleven-year-old. Development is too complex to be reduced to milestones or benchmarks showing 'where one is', and it is certainly too closely related to the task set to be reduced to a single score.

We have found no evidence for a linear progression of skills (except in certain one-off achievements in the early years such as knowledge of alphabetical order). Instead, we have evidence to show the recursive nature of writing, with children returning time and again to similar tasks, refining their ability on each return. One example which demonstrates this point comes from an Infant class whose members had produced stories for younger children. They decided to write autobiographical notes on the back cover and came up with texts such as:

This child has captured an autobiographical style, appropriately using the third person. She will, however, be likely to revisit such tasks, improving her performance each time.

While criticism is levelled at any assessment which assumes some age-related, incremental growth in writing, this is not to dismiss the need for criteria. Teachers need to be able to look critically at children's texts and to judge what constitutes the best report, the best story or the best argument. The criteria should be made explicit to the pupil and to the wider audience.

We would suggest that the best way to demonstrate a writer's development is to provide examples from a number of different tasks. These should be supported by a commentary which makes clear the context in which they were produced and the criteria by which they were judged.

5 Who should be responsible for assessing development?

Assessment needs to be an integral part of learning rather than an imposed, artificial constraint. To ensure that this happens with writing, teachers in the Project have found it important:

a that teachers are not the sole evaluators of writing

b that the children themselves monitor development

For **(a)**, teachers have ensured that writing is assessed, where possible, by the audience for whom it was intended. For example, an information booklet for younger children would be assessed by its readers.

For **(b)**, pupils have been given responsibility for looking at their own development and that of others.

A child aged six who can discuss another child's writing . . .

'I liked the Bitt when you fell over and I liked it when you buried the wolf. Becose it was funny — I liked it when fell dawn and went home

The Magic Book by Stephen
This wrtg by Helen'

. . . is more likely to become a critical and reflective writer than is a child accustomed to receiving only a teacher's response.

Teachers, too, need to be observers of their own development so that they can answer questions such as *'Are we doing our job better now?'* One teacher who was interviewed as part of the Project's own evaluation reflected thus:

'Well, I think just the whole way they approach education — the whole business of what happens in a school — (This is a hard one, isn't it?) For example, pupils are assessing themselves, very much so at each stage. . . If you were assessing yourself, what would you put on the piece of paper? We talked about how people assess. They said although they'd all like to have "good", they would like to know why it was good — what part of it, why the teacher thought it was good, and when I asked why, they said because it would tell you which things to do next time. . . I certainly wouldn't have dreamed of talking about assessment like that before. I don't think it would have come within my orbit before . . . with Art or Science, whatever we are doing, it sort of goes right across the board. I think this is the bonus, that they are looking at everything — you are not just doing one piece of work that comes under a category, as it used to on the timetable, as English for example, you are giving them . . . a way of looking at all the different aspects of education.'

6 What is the role of writing in the curriculum?

The assessment of writing is usually discussed in terms which falsely ascribe a homogeneity to writing, and which suggest that the purpose of writing in school is to reflect what is known: reports of experiments; accounts of trips; reviews of work read. Central to the Project's thinking is the role of writing to develop hypotheses, to sort out ideas, to jot down fleeting images.

The spider leg.

1.) I was suprised that the leg looked like that close up.

2.) I was talking to the teacher about the hair a bout if it is different to our hair & discuvererd that it was really part of the shell it was spikes

3.) when you loked thew the telescope it was solid and our hair is hollow unlike the hair on the leg. It is that the hair is grown from a balb.

The use of writing as a tool for learning as well as a reflection of that learning needs to be reinforced in all subjects and to be considered in assessments of the writing opportunities provided for children.

7   How can abilities be communicated?

Parents, employers and other teachers in the school (and in other schools) need to know how a child is progressing. Given what has been stated above, we see no benefit in providing results from decontextualised tests. We would advocate procedures which show what a child can do, how that was achieved and what further opportunities need to be provided to ensure future development.

We have examples within the Project of:

- parents being introduced to ways of looking at a child's writing which will demonstrate his/her strengths

For example, in a number of local authorities, parents have been involved in evening workshops where they look at children's writing, discuss their responses and think about ways in which they might develop writing activities with their children at home.

- parents being involved in the formulation of assessment policies and working alongside teachers in the support of their child's development

The value of consulting parents when assessment policies are being discussed has been highlighted in many schools. Such involvement has led to parents having more understanding of the process of curriculum development and of their children's learning processes.

- teachers looking at ways in which they can communicate a child's development to a new school not simply through a transfer record of some kind but also by providing the contexts in which such writing has been/ could be promoted

For example, in one authority, children transferring from the Primary school take with them the beginnings of a folder on 'Myself' containing many different types of writing. Work on this folder is continued in their new class. The Secondary teachers thus both see what each child has been achieving and ensure that continuity is maintained. In another authority, each child is monitored by means of a literacy card which is discussed at joint meetings of Primary and Secondary teachers.

- employers working alongside teachers, discussing their priorities and the types of example which would help them make selections

The National Writing Project has initiated a number of activities to promote closer links between school and work.

8   What support do teachers need?

Curriculum development and innovations in methods of assessment need to be supported by specific in-service training as well as by provision of time and resources for teachers to consider changes. The clearest message from all the Project's wide-ranging work is that teachers want to be made part of any development and need structures in which they can reflect on and exchange ideas and refine their practice. If long-term assessment procedures are to be introduced, this need for support will be especially strong.